Why Animals Don't Get Heart Attacks – But People Do!

D1337487

"New thoughts and new truths go through three stages. First they are ridiculed. Next they are violently opposed. Then, finally they are accepted as being self evident."

Arthur Schopenhauer

Matthias Rath, M.D.

Why Animals Don't Get Heart Attacks

... But People Do!

The Discovery That Will Eradicate Heart Disease

Natural prevention of heart attacks, strokes, high blood pressure, diabetes, high cholesterol and many other cardiovascular risks

This bestseller is the focus of a new health care system

ISBN 90 76332 03 7

2nd Edition

Branch UK
17 Liverpool Road
Slough
SL 14 QZ
Fax: 017-53-690069
www.rath.co.uk

Table of Contents

Introduction

International Declaration:

> ### We, the People of the World, Declare the 21st Century "The Century of Eradicating Heart Disease"
>
> **Only once in the course of human events** comes the time when heart attacks, strokes and other cardiovascular conditions can be eradicated. This time is now. Just as the discovery that micro-organisms are the cause of infectious diseases led to the control of infectious epidemics, so will the discovery that heart attacks and strokes are the result of long-term vitamin deficiencies lead to the control of the cardiovascular epidemic. Mankind can eradicate heart disease as a major cause of death and disability during the 21st century.
>
> **Animals don't get heart attacks** because they produce vitamin C in their bodies, which protects their blood vessel walls. In humans, unable to produce vitamin C, dietary vitamin deficiency weakens these walls. Cardiovascular disease is an early form of scurvy. Clinical studies document that optimum daily intake of vitamins and other essential nutrients halts and reverses coronary heart disease naturally. These essential nutrients supply vital bioenergy to millions of heart and blood vessel cells, thereby optimizing cardiovascular functions. Optimum supply of vitamins and other essential nutrients can prevent and help correct cardiovascular conditions naturally. Heart attacks, strokes, high blood pressure conditions, irregular heartbeat, heart failure, circulatory problems in diabetes, and other cardiovascular problems, will be essentially unknown in future generations.
>
> **Eradicating heart disease** is the next great goal uniting all mankind. The availability of vitamins and other essential nutrients needed to control the global cardiovascular epidemic is unlimited. The eradication of heart disease is dependent on one single factor: How fast can we spread the message that vitamins and other essential nutrients are the solution to the cardiovascular epidemic.

21st Century: Century of eradicating Heart Disease

The main hurdles we have to overcome are the interests of pharmaceutical companies and other special interest groups which are trying to block the spread of this life-saving information in order to protect a global prescription drug market. But the health interests of millions of people are more important than the stock price of any drug company. We, the people of the world, recognize that we have to protect our health interests and that the eradication of heart disease is dependent upon our joint efforts.

We, people of all nations, races and religions; local, regional and national governments and other public and private organizations; health insurers, health maintenance organizations, hospitals, medical offices and other health care providers; churches, schools, businesses and other community groups recognize our historic opportunity and responsibility to act now – for our generation and for all generations to come:

- **We proclaim the 21st Century the "Century of Eradicating Heart Disease".**

- **We will spread information about the life-saving benefits of vitamins.**

- **We invite everyone to join us in winning one of the greatest victories of mankind.**

A hundred years ago: Eradicating epidemics

For millennia infectious diseases were the number one cause of death and billions of people have died of it.

For millennia people believed that the cause of these epidemics is a curse of heaven.

Then,150 years ago Louis Pasteur discovered that these epidemics are caused by bacteria and other micro-organisms.

This discovery enabled the implementation of preventive methods as well as the development of vaccines and antibiotics.

A few years ago the World Health Organization (WHO) declared the first infectious disease, smallpox, as eradicated.

Today: Eradicating heart disease

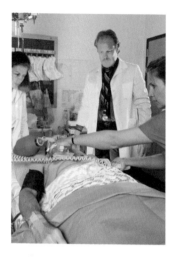

During the 20th century, cardiovascular diseases became the number one cause of death in the industrialized world. Worldwide over a billion people have died during this century from heart attacks and strokes.

Because the main cause of cardiovascular disease has remained unknown until now, the cardiovascular epidemic continues to spread on a global scale.

This book documents the solution to the cardiovascular epidemic: Animals don't get heart attacks, because – as opposed to humans – they produce their own vitamin C in their bodies. Heart attacks and strokes are not diseases but the consequence of chronic vitamin deficiency and therefore preventable.

How You Can Immediately Benefit from Reading This Book

This book summarizes for the first time the medical break-through in the area of vitamins and cardiovascular health:

Why animals don't get heart attacks, but every second man and woman dies from one. Animals don't get heart attacks because they produce large amounts of vitamin C in their bodies. Vitamin C optimizes the production of collagen and other reinforcement molecules, thereby stabilizing the walls of the arteries and preventing atherosclerotic deposits, heart attacks, and strokes. We human beings cannot manufacture a single molecule of vitamin C in our bodies and, in addition, frequently get too few vitamins in our diet. The inevitable consequence is a weakening of the artery walls and atherosclerosis. Chronic vitamin deficiency is the main cause for the epidemic spread of cardiovascular disease.

The scientific breakthrough in the control of cardiovascular disease. Heart attacks and strokes are not diseases; they are caused by vitamin deficiencies. Currently, every second man and woman dies from cardiovascular disease, but heart attacks and strokes will essentially be unknown in future generations. This book is the original account of the medical breakthrough that will eventually liberate mankind from the cardiovascular epidemic.

The World's first patented therapy for the natural reversal of cardiovascular disease. This book presents the world's first patented therapy for the reversal of atherosclerotic deposits without angioplasty or bypass surgery. Once the artery wall is weakened by vitamin deficiency, millions of fat particles (lipoproteins) are deposited in the artery wall by means of biological "adhesive tapes," eventually leading to atherosclerosis, heart attacks, and strokes. These atherosclerotic deposits can now be largely prevented and reversed with natural "Teflon" agents, which neutralize these adhesive properties. The first generation of artery wall "Teflon" agents are the natural amino acids lysine and proline, which become even more effective in combination with other vitamins. Thus, an old dream of mankind becomes reality: the natural reversal of cardiovascular disease.

The World's leading cardiovascular health program is - based on these breakthrough discoveries - a scientifically based nutritional supplement program. Dr. Rath's Vitamin Program includes a selection of essential vitamins, minerals, and natural amino acids in combination with a healthy lifestyle. The essential nutrient program was developed as a daily supplement for men and women at any age to protect the cardiovascular system in a natural way. Tens of thousands of people are already following this program for prevention and adjunct therapy. This book documents the profound health benefits of this program even with the most severe health conditions such as angina pectoris, irregular heartbeat, heart failure, diabetes, high blood pressure, after a heart attack, coronary bypass surgery, angioplasty and many others. Thus, it is not surprising that Dr. Rath's Vitamin Program is today's leading cardiovascular health program with patients in many countries around the world following it.

The World's first vitamin program to document total disappearance of coronary atherosclerosis. Dr. Rath's Vitamin Program is the world's first natural health program to halt and to actually reverse existing coronary artery deposits. Drug companies selling cholesterol-lowering drugs and diet prophets have been making similar claims without substantiation. A growing number of people deceived by these false claims are left with more damage to their health than benefit. This book documents unequivocally that only a vitamin-based program provides the decisive bioenergy for the cells of the artery walls to initiate the healing process. For the first time in the history of medicine you will actually see proof that coronary deposits, the cause of heart attacks, can entirely disappear in a natural way. By using Dr. Rath's Vitamin Program, physicians and patients alike now have an effective natural alternative to bypass surgery, angioplasty and other conventional treatments of cardiovascular disease.

An ounce of prevention is worth a pound of cure. Above all, this book gives you practical recommendations to prevent cardiovascular health problems in the first place. This natural cardiovascular health program is an effective, safe, and affordable way for men and women of all ages to help prevent cardiovascular diseases. Based on this natural health program, millions of people today and future generations will not have to wait until cardiovascular problems develop.

This book is an authentic report of one of the greatest breakthroughs in medicine. This book is written by the scientist and physician who led this medical advance from its beginning. The last chapters document the decisive discoveries, the development of an entirely new understanding of the origins of heart disease, and the early support by two-time Nobel Laureate, Linus Pauling. You will also read how the scientific discoveries of this book triggered one of the largest battles in the history of the United States - the "1992-1994 Battle for Vitamin Freedom". It documents the historic victory millions of Americans gained over the FDA and the pharmaceutical industry. Passage of the Nutritional Health and Education Act of August 1994, finally allowed health information in connection with vitamins to be freely disseminated.

This book has the pharmaceutical companies run amok. The annual market for cardiovascular prescription drugs in the US alone is over 100 billion dollars. Unable to fight the scientific truth of Dr. Rath's discoveries and the fact that animals don't get heart attacks because they make their own vitamin C, the pharmaceutical companies have embarked on a worldwide effort to block the spreading of this book and its information. Towards this end they even formed an international Cartel named "Codex Alimentarius" to outlaw all health claims in relation to vitamins for all member countries of the UN worldwide. This book also tells you why, among all countries, the German government is politically spearheading these unethical efforts and how the people in Germany have already delivered a decisive blow to the Codex-Cartel.

This book is the starting point of a new health care system. Hundreds of thousands of Dr. Rath's books have been sold around the world. They introduced an entirely new understanding of health and disease, which enables millions of people to take responsibility for their own body and health. This book will bring about a new health care system based on the following cornerstones: health education of the people at large will replace unhealthy dependence on health experts; primary and community-based health care will replace high-tech medicine; effective natural therapies will replace deadlocks in conventional medicine; medical research focused on prevention and eradication of diseases will replace the development of pharmaceutical drugs that treat symptoms but do not cure. This book is the starting point of a new health care system.

Take your health in your own hands. Millions of people now realize that they have to defend their health and their lives against the financial interests of the unscrupulous Pharma-Cartel. To overcome these unethical forces as quickly as possible, millions of patients and people world-wide have to take responsibility for their own health. This book is a manual of what you can do to help bring about this global change in health care that will save millions of lives. Most importantly, you should talk about this book with your friends, neighbors and colleagues, thereby helping to overcome the information boycott imposed by the Pharma-Cartel on this medical breakthrough. Of course, you are also invited to join our international network of health consultants, a unique opportunity to help other people and start a new and fulfilling career.

The 10-Step Program for Optimum Cardiovascular Health

The medical breakthrough documented in this book can be summarized in a practical 10-step-program of essential nutrients:

1 **Be aware of the size and function of your cardiovascular system.**
   Did you know that your blood vessel pipeline system measures 60,000 miles and is the largest organ in your body? Did you know that your heart pumps 100,000 times every day, performing the greatest amount of work of all organs? Optimizing your cardiovascular health benefits your entire body and your overall health. Because your body is as old as your cardiovascular system, optimizing your cardiovascular health adds years to your life.

2 **Stabilize the walls of your blood vessels.**
   Blood vessel instability and lesions in your blood vessel walls are the primary causes for cardiovascular disease. Vitamin C is the cement of the blood vessel walls and stabilizes them. Animals don't get heart disease because they produce enough endogenous vitamin C in their livers to protect their blood vessels. In contrast, we humans develop deposits leading to heart attacks and strokes because we cannot manufacture endogenous vitamin C and generally get too few vitamins in our diet.

3 **Reverse existing deposits in your arteries without surgery.**
   Cholesterol and fat particles are deposited inside the blood vessel walls by means of biological adhesives. "Teflon"-like agents can prevent this stickiness. The amino acids lysine and proline are Nature's "Teflon" agents. Together with vitamin C, they help reverse existing deposits naturally.

4 Relax your blood vessel walls.

Deposits and spasms of the blood vessel walls are the causes of high blood pressure. Dietary supplementation of magnesium (Nature's calcium antagonist) and vitamin C relax the blood vessel walls and normalize high blood pressure. The natural amino acid arginine can be of additional value.

5 Optimize the performance of your heart.

The heart is the motor of the cardiovascular system. Like the motor of your car, millions of muscle cells need cell fuel for optimum performance. Nature's cell fuels include carnitine, coenzyme Q-10, B vitamins, and many other nutrients and trace elements. Dietary supplementation of these essential nutrients will optimize the pumping performance of the heart and contribute to regular heartbeat.

6   **Protect your cardiovascular pipelines from rusting.**
Biological rusting, or oxidation, damages your cardiovascular system and accelerates the aging process. Vitamin C, vitamin E, beta-carotene, and selenium are the most important natural antioxidants. Other important antioxidants are bioflavonoids, such as pycnogenol. Dietary supplementation of these antioxidants provides important rust protection for your cardiovascular system. Above all, stop smoking, because cigarette smoke accelerates the biological rusting of your blood vessels.

7   **Exercise regularly.**
Regular physical activity is another important step for optimum cardiovascular health. Moderate regular exercise like walking or bicycling is ideal and can be performed by everybody.

8   **Eat a prudent diet.**
The diet of our ancestors over thousands of generations was rich in plant nutrition and high in fiber and vitamins. These dietary preferences shaped the metabolism of our bodies today. A diet rich in fruits and vegetables and low in fat and sugars enhances your cardiovascular health.

9   **Find time to relax.**
Physical and emotional stresses are cardiovascular risk factors. Schedule hours and days to relax as you would schedule your appointments. You should also know that the production of the stress hormone adrenaline uses up your body's vitamin C supply. Long-term physical or emotional stress depletes your body's vitamin pool and requires dietary vitamin supplementation.

10 Start now.

Thickening of the blood vessel walls is not only a problem of the elderly, it starts early in life. Studies have shown that first blood vessel deposits can develop in the second decade of life. Start protecting your cardiovascular system now. The earlier you start, the more years you will have.

Dr. Rath's Vitamin Program

CELLULAR MEDICINE - BASIC PROGRAM

The basic formula of Dr. Raths vitamin program consists of more than 30 vitamins, minerals, amino acids and trace elements. These essential nutrients have been selected according to scientific criteria and their main function as bioenergy poviders to a multitude of cells of the human body. This *basic* cellular medicine program was developed as a daily nutritional supplement for everyone in order to optimize cardiovascular health and to help prevent cardiovascular and other health problems. The first number gives the daily minimum of each nutrient for a healthy adult person. Patients and other people with special needs can double or triple these amounts.

CELLULAR MEDICINE - SPECIAL PROGRAMS

For patients with certain heart conditions – such as coronary heart disease, high blood pressure, diabetes, heart failure and others – *special* cellular medicine programs are recommended in addition to the basic vitamin programm. These *special* cellular medicine programs contain certain essential nutrients in higher ammounts or in addition to those contained in the *basic* program.

The health benefits of this program are documented throughout this book and in an additional comprehensive testimonial book: "Good Health is Possible!"

BASIC CELLULAR MEDICINE PROGRAM

VITAMINS

Vitamin C	600 - 3,000	mg
Vitamin E (d-alpha-Tocopherol)	130 - 600	I.U.
Beta-Carotene	1,600 - 8,000	I.U.
Vitamin B-1 (Thiamine)	5 - 40	mg
Vitamin B-2 (Riboflavin)	5 - 40	mg
Vitamin B-3 (Nicotinate)	45 - 200	mg
Vitamin B-5 (Pantothenate)	40 - 200	mg
Vitamin B-6 (Pyridoxine)	10 - 50	mg
Vitamin B-12(Cyanocobalamin)	20 - 100	mcg
Vitamin D-3	100 - 600	I.U.
Folic Acid	90 - 400	mcg
Biotin	60 - 300	mcg

MINERALS

Calcium	30 - 150	mg
Magnesium	40 - 200	mg
Potassium	20 - 90	mg
Phosphate	10 - 60	mg

TRACE ELEMENTS

Zinc	5 - 30	mg
Manganese	1 - 6	mg
Copper	300 - 2,000	mcg
Selenium	20 - 100	mcg
Chromium	10 - 50	mcg
Molybdenum	4 - 20	mcg

OTHER IMPORTANT NUTRIENTS

L-Proline	100 - 500	mg
L-Lysine	100 - 500	mg
L-Carnitine	30 - 150	mg
L-Arginine	40 - 150	mg
L-Cysteine	30 - 150	mg
Inositol	30 - 150	mg
Coenzyme Q-10	5 - 30	mg
Pycnogenol	5 - 30	mg
Bioflavonoids	100 - 450	mg

Dr. Rath's Vitamin Program Brings Biological Fuel To Millions of Cardiovascular Cells

Throughout this book you will read remarkable health improvements from people following Dr. Rath's Vitamin Program. The scientific basis of these dramatic health improvements can be summarized as follows: the cells in our body fulfill a multitude of different functions. Gland cells produce hormones; white blood cells produce antibodies; heart muscle cells generate and conduct biological electricity for the heart beat. The specific function of each cell is determined by the genetic software program, the genes located in each cell core.

Despite these different functions, it is important to understand that all cells use the same carriers of bioenergy and the same biocatalysts for a multitude of biochemical reactions inside these cells. Many of these essential biocatalysts and bioenergy molecules cannot be produced by the body itself and have to be supplemented in our diet on a regular basis. Vitamins, certain amino acids, minerals, and trace elements are among the most important essential nutrients for optimum function of each cell. Without optimum intake of these essential nutrients, the function of millions of cells becomes impaired and diseases develop.

Unfortunately, conventional medicine still does not recognize the decisive role of vitamins and other essential nutrients for optimum cellular function and for optimum health. The modern concept of Cellular Medicine fundamentally changes that. In a few years, the daily supplementation with Dr. Rath's Vitamin Program will be a matter of course for everyone, just like eating and drinking.

Single cell (schematic)

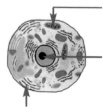

**Cellular Power Plant
(Mitochondrium)**

**Cellular Core
Central Unit
(Nucleus)**

**Cellular Production Line
(Endoplasmic Reticulum)**

Important Biocatalysts:

- **Vitamin C**
- **Vitamin B-1**
- **Vitamin B-3**
- **Vitamin B-5**
- **Vitamin B-6**
- **Vitamin B-12**

- **Carnitine**
- **Coenzyme Q-10**
- **Minerals**
- **Trace elements**

The metabolic software program
of each cell is exactly determined
by the genetic information in each
cell core. Essential nutrients are
needed as biocatalysts and as
carriers of bioenergy in each cell.
Both functions are essential for
optimum performance of millions
of cells.

Dr. Rath's Vitamin Program – Biological Fuel for Millions of Cells

25

Cellular Medicine:
The Solution to Cardiovascular Disease

The most profound impact of Cellular Medicine will be in the area of cardiovascular health because this is the most active organ system of our body and therefore has the highest consumption of essential nutrients. The opposite page illustrates the most important cells of the cardiovascular system.

Cells of the blood vessel walls: The endothelial cells form the barrier or protective layer between the blood and the blood vessel wall; moreover, these cells contribute to a variety of metabolic functions, such as optimum blood viscosity. The smooth muscle cells produce collagen and other reinforcement molecules, providing optimum stability and tone to the blood vessel walls.

The cells of the heart muscle: The main role of heart muscle cells is the pumping function to maintain blood circulation. A subtype of heart muscle cell is specialized and capable of generating and conducting biological electricity for the heartbeat.

The blood cells: Even the millions of blood corpuscles circulating in the bloodstream are nothing other than cells. They are responsible for transport of oxygen, defense, scavenging, wound healing, and many other functions. The following pages describe how deficiencies in vitamins and other essential nutrients in these different cell types are closely associated with the most frequent cardiovascular diseases today.

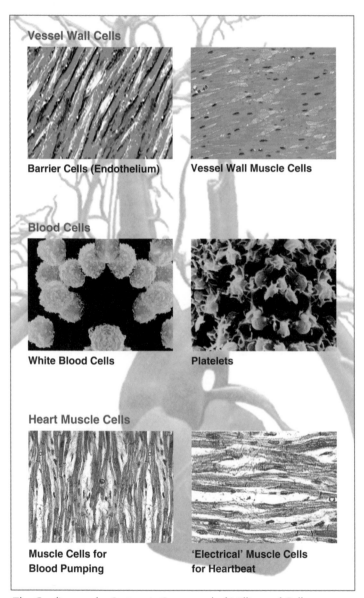

Vessel Wall Cells

Barrier Cells (Endothelium)   **Vessel Wall Muscle Cells**

Blood Cells

White Blood Cells   **Platelets**

Heart Muscle Cells

Muscle Cells for   **'Electrical' Muscle Cells**
Blood Pumping   **for Heartbeat**

The Cardiovascular System Is Composed of Millions of Cells

Vitamin Deficiency in Artery Wall Cells Causes Heart Attacks, Strokes, and High Blood Pressure

Long-term deficiency of vitamins and other essential nutrients in millions of vascular wall cells impairs the function of the blood vessel walls. The most frequent consequences are high blood pressure conditions and the development of atherosclerotic deposits which lead to heart attacks and strokes.

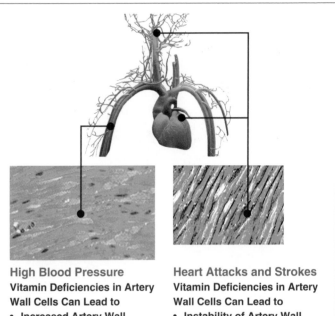

High Blood Pressure
Vitamin Deficiencies in Artery Wall Cells Can Lead to
- **Increased Artery Wall Tension**
- **Narrowing of Artery Diameter**
- **Thickening of Artery Walls and, Thereby, to High Blood Pressure**

Heart Attacks and Strokes
Vitamin Deficiencies in Artery Wall Cells Can Lead to
- **Instability of Artery Wall**
- **Lesion, Cracks**
- **Atherosclerotic Deposits and, Thereby, to Heart Attacks and Strokes**

Vitamin Deficiency in Heart Muscle Cells Causes Irregular Heartbeat and Heart Failure

A chronic deficiency of vitamins and other essential nutrients in millions of heart muscle cells can contribute to an impaired heart function. The most frequent consequences are irregular heartbeat (arrhythmia) and heart failure (shortness of breath, edema, and fatigue).

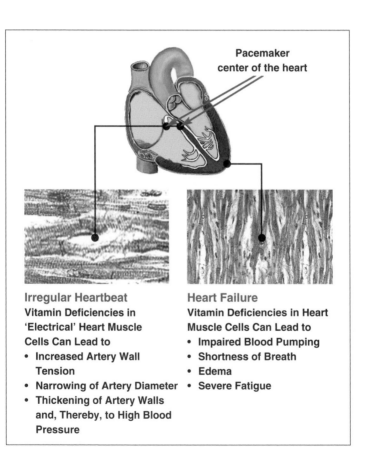

Pacemaker center of the heart

Irregular Heartbeat
Vitamin Deficiencies in 'Electrical' Heart Muscle Cells Can Lead to
- Increased Artery Wall Tension
- Narrowing of Artery Diameter
- Thickening of Artery Walls and, Thereby, to High Blood Pressure

Heart Failure
Vitamin Deficiencies in Heart Muscle Cells Can Lead to
- Impaired Blood Pumping
- Shortness of Breath
- Edema
- Severe Fatigue

Notes

Atherosclerosis, Heart attack and Stroke

2

Dr. Rath's Vitamin program
for Prevention and Adjunct Therapy

The Facts About Coronary Heart Disease

How Dr. Rath's Vitamin Program Can Help Patients With Coronary Heart Disease

Clinical Studies Document Prevention of Cardiovascular Disease with Vitamins

Background Information for Dr. Rath's Vitamin Program and Cardiovascular Disease

The Facts About Coronary Heart Disease

- **Every second man and woman** in the industrialized world dies from the consequences of atherosclerotic deposits in the coronary arteries (leading to heart attack) or in the arteries supplying blood to the brain (leading to stroke). The epidemic spread of these cardiovascular diseases is largely due to the fact that until now the true nature of atherosclerosis and coronary heart disease has been insufficiently understood.

- **Conventional medicine** is largely confined to treating the symptoms of this disease. Calcium antagonists, beta-blockers, nitrates, and other drugs are prescribed to alleviate angina pain. Surgical procedures (angioplasty, bypass surgery) are applied to improve blood flow mechanically. Hardly any conventional medicine targets the underlying problem: the instability of the vascular wall which triggers the development of atherosclerotic deposits.

- **Cellular Medicine** provides a breakthrough in our understanding of these causes and leads to effective prevention and treatment of coronary heart disease. The primary cause of coronary heart disease and other forms of atherosclerotic disease is a chronic deficiency in vitamins and other essential nutrients in millions of vascular wall cells. This leads to instability of the vascular walls, to lesions and cracks, to atherosclerotic deposits, and eventually to heart attacks or strokes. Since the primary cause of cardiovascular disease is a deficiency of essential nutrients in the vascular wall, a daily optimum intake of these essential nutrients is the primary measure to prevent atherosclerosis and to help repair wall damage.

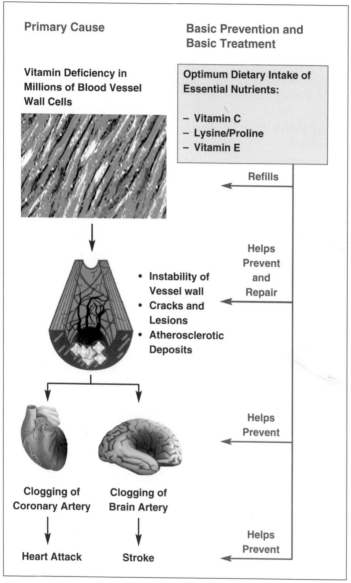

Primary Cause

Basic Prevention and Basic Treatment

Vitamin Deficiency in Millions of Blood Vessel Wall Cells

Optimum Dietary Intake of Essential Nutrients:

 – **Vitamin C**
 – **Lysine/Proline**
 – **Vitamin E**

Refills

 • **Instability of Vessel wall**
 • **Cracks and Lesions**
 • **Atherosclerotic Deposits**

Helps Prevent and Repair

Clogging of Coronary Artery

Clogging of Brain Artery

Helps Prevent

Heart Attack

Stroke

Helps Prevent

Coronary Artery Disease And Other Forms of Atherosclerotic Cardiovascular Disease

- **Scientific research and clinical studies** have already documented the particular value of vitamin C, vitamin E, beta carotene, lysine, proline, and other ingredients of Dr. Rath's Vitamin Program in the prevention of cardiovascular disease and in improving the health of patients with existing cardiovascular disease.

- **Dr. Rath's Vitamin Program** comprises selected essential nutrients to help prevent cardiovascular disease naturally and to help repair existing damage. The following pages document health improvements from patients with coronary heart disease and other forms of cardiovascular disease, who have benefited from this program.

- **My recommendation for patients** with cardiovascular disease is to start immediately with this natural cardiovascular program and inform your doctor about it. Follow Dr. Rath's Vitamin Program in addition to your medication. Vitamin C and E are natural "blood thinners." If you are on blood thinning medication you should talk to your doctor about the vitamins you take so that additional blood tests can be performed and your prescription medication may be decreased. Do not change any medication without consulting your doctor.

- **Prevention is better than treatment.** The success of this essential nutrient program in patients with existing atherosclerosis and cardiovascular disease is based on the fact that the millions of cardiovascular cells are replenished with cell fuel for optimum cell function. A natural cardiovascular program able to correct an existing health condition is, of course, your best choice to prevent this condition in the first place.

Dr. Rath's Vitamin Program Can Halt and Reverse Coronary Heart Disease

Millions of people die every year from heart attacks because no effective treatment to halt or reverse coronary artery disease has been available. Therefore, we decided to test the efficacy of Dr. Rath's Vitamin Program for the Number One health problem of our time: coronary atherosclerosis, the cause of heart attacks. If this nutritional supplement program is able to stop further growth of coronary atherosclerosis, the fight against heart attacks can be won and the goal of eradicating heart disease becomes reality.

To measure the success of our vitamin program we did not primarily look at risk factors circulating in the blood stream. We focused directly on the key problem, the atherosclerotic deposits inside the walls of the coronary arteries. A fascinating new diagnostic technique had just become available that allowed us to measure the size of the coronary deposits non-invasively: Ultrafast Computed Tomography.

Ultrafast CT, the "mammogram of the heart," is a new diagnostic technology that allows non-invasive testing for coronary artery disease.

35

The Ultrafast CT measures areas and density of the calcium deposits without any needles or radioactive dye involved; then the computer automatically calculates their size by determining the Coronary Artery Scan (CAS) score. The higher the CAS score, the more calcium has accumulated, indicating more advanced coronary artery disease. Compared to angiography and treadmill tests, Ultrafast CT is the most precise diagnostic technique available today to detect coronary artery disease already in its early stage. This diagnostic test allows detection of deposits in coronary arteries long before a patient notices any angina pectoris or other symptoms. Moreover, since it measures directly the deposits in the artery walls, it is a much better indicator for a person's cardiovascular risk than any

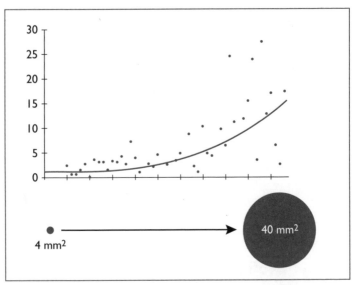

Growth Rate of Coronary Deposits Per Year in Each Patient
Without Dr. Rath's Vitamin Program the atherosclerotic plaques in the coronary arteries increased exponentially. This picture shows the growth rate of coronary deposits in each patient before the vitamin program started. Patients with early coronary artery disease had an average increase of plaque area of 4 mm² every year (left side of the figure). The deposits of patients with advanced coronary artery disease increased by 40 mm² and more every year (right side).

measurements of cholesterol or other risk factors in the blood-stream.

We studied 55 patients with various degrees of coronary artery disease. Changes in the size of the coronary artery calcifications in each patient were measured over an average period of one year without Dr. Rath's Vitamin Program, followed by a period of one year with the vitamin program. In this way, the heart scans of the same person could be compared without and with the vitamin program. This study design had the advantage that the patients served as their own controls. The dosages of essential nutrients given were about the amounts listed in the right column of the vitamin table at the beginning of this book.

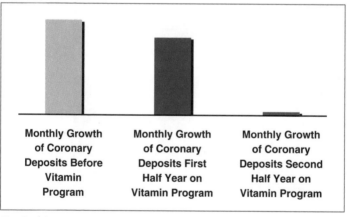

| Monthly Growth of Coronary Deposits Before Vitamin Program | Monthly Growth of Coronary Deposits First Half Year on Vitamin Program | Monthly Growth of Coronary Deposits Second Half Year on Vitamin Program |

Dr. Rath's Vitamin Program Stops Coronary Heart Disease Before You Even Feel It.
With Dr. Rath's Vitamin Program the fast growth of coronary artery deposits could be slowed down during the first half year and essentially stopped within the second half year. Thus, no heart attacks can develop. These are the study results from patients with early coronary deposit who, like millions of adults in the prime of their lives, have developed heart disease without yet feeling it.

The results of this landmark study were published in the *Journal of Applied Nutrition* in 1996 (see reference listing at the end of this book). The most important findings are also presented here. This study measured for the first time how aggressive coronary artery disease grows until eventually a heart attack occurs. Without Dr. Rath's Vitamin Program, the coronary calcifications increased at an exponential rate, with an average growth of 44% every year. Thus, without vitamin pro-

Without Vitamin Program

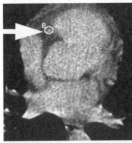 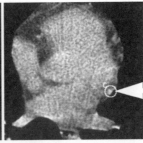

Deposits in two Coronary Arteries

With Vitamin Program

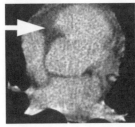 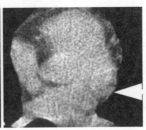

Deposits In Both Arteries Disappeared Naturally

Dr. Rath's Vitamin Program Is the World's First Therapy Documenting Natural Disappearance of Coronary Deposits.
These pictures document a milestone in medicine – the complete natural disappearance of coronary heart disease. The Ultrafast Computer Tomography (Ultrafast CT) pictures (top row) document atherosclerotic deposits in the right and left coronary arteries of this patient. After about one year on Dr. Rath's Vitamin Program these coronary deposits have entirely disappeared – indicating a natural healing process of the artery wall.

tection, coronary deposits add about half their size every year. When patients started Dr. Rath's Vitamin Program, this trend was reversed and the average growth rate of coronary calcifications actually slowed down. Most significantly, in patients with early stages of coronary heart disease, this essential nutrient program stopped further growth of coronary heart disease within one year. Thus, this study also gives us valuable information about the time it takes until Dr. Rath's Vitamin Program shows its natural healing effect on the artery wall. While for the first six months the deposits in these patients continued to grow, although at a decreased pace, the growth essentially stops during the second six months on this vitamin program. Of course, any therapy that stops coronary artery disease in its early stages prevents heart attacks later on.

It is not surprising that there is a delay of several months until the healing effect of Dr. Rath's Vitamin Program on the artery

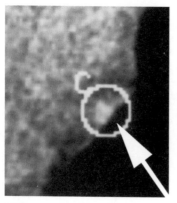 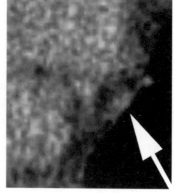

Before   **After**

Natural Healing of Coronary Artery Disease
Before Dr. Rath's Vitamin Program the patient had developed athero-sclerotic deposits in the walls of his left coronary artery (white circled area in the left picture). The above pictures are magnifications from the heart scan X-ray pictures taken with the computer tomograph.

39

wall becomes noticeable. Atherosclerotic deposits develop over many years or decades, and it takes several months to control this aggressive disease and start the healing process. More advanced stages of coronary heart disease may take still longer before the vascular healing process is measurable. To answer these questions, we are continuing this study.

Can already existing coronary deposits be reversed in a natural way? The answer is yes. In individual patients we documented natural reversal and complete disappearance of early coronary artery deposits within about one year. The ongoing study will tell us how long the natural reversal takes in patients with advanced coronary artery disease.

The complete natural disappearance with Dr. Rath's Vitamin Program documents that this vitamin program contains the essential ingredients to start a natural healing process of the artery wall.

In patients with *early* coronary heart disease, this healing of the artery wall can lead to the complete natural removal of athero-sclerotic deposits (see above).
In patients with *advanced* coronary artery disease, Dr. Rath's Vitamin Program can stabilize the artery walls, halt the further growth of the coronary deposits, and reverse them, at least in part; thus contributing to the prevention of heart attacks.

Improving Human Health World-Wide

Our clinical study marks a major breakthrough in medicine and will lead to health improvements for millions of people throughout the world. For the first time, the following clinical results were documented:

- **Without vitamin therapy, coronary artery disease is a** very aggressive disease and the deposits grow on average at a staggering rate of 44% per year.

- **Dr. Rath's Vitamin Program is proven to halt coronary** atherosclerosis, the cause of heart attacks, already in its early stages.

- **Thus, there now exists an effective natural therapy to** prevent and to reverse coronary heart disease naturally – without angioplasty or bypass surgery.

- **Every man and every woman in any country of the world** can immediately take advantage of this medical breakthrough.

- **During the next decades, deaths from heart attacks and** strokes will be reduced to a fraction of their current toll and cardiovascular disease will essentially be unknown to future generations.

This Study Calls for Immediate Action:

- **Every reader of this book should make use of this life-**saving information and forward it to friends, colleagues and to the community.

- **Doctors and other health professionals should inform** their patients.

- **Health insurance companies and health maintenance** organizations, as well as public health strategies should take immediate advantage of this medical breakthrough.

How Dr. Rath's Vitamin Program Can Help Patients With Coronary Heart Disease

These pages document letters from coronary heart disease patients who have followed Dr. Rath's Vitamin Program. This essential nutrient program improved the health of these patients and their quality of life beyond anything possible before. Please share this important information with anyone you know who suffers from cardiovascular disease.

Dear Dr. Rath:

In August, 1990, at the age of 20, I was diagnosed with viral cardiomyopathy. My doctors informed me that my only hope for survival would be a heart transplant. In November 1990, I was transported to the hospital for **heart transplant surgery.**

As part of my post-operative treatment, I go into the hospital for an annual heart catheterization. Up until January 1995, my heart caths were fine. In January, 1995, I had a heart catheterization and my cardiologist found four blockages; **three (coronary artery) vessels were approximately 90% occluded (blocked) and the fourth vessel was approximately 60% occluded.** *I had also gained one hundred pounds since the transplant and my cardiologist was furious. I was instructed to begin a strict low-fat diet immediately. In May, 1995, I was introduced to your cardiovascular vitamin program. I had lost 30 pounds on my low-fat diet and began using your formulas.* **I had a repeat catheterization in November, 1995.**

The results were phenomenal!! This cath showed that the three occlusions previously at approximately 90% were reduced by approximately 50% and the fourth occlusion previously at approximately 60% had no obstruction at all. *The other exciting news was that I had also lost an additional 50 pounds for a total of 80 pounds!! All of this occurred in six months. These formulas have dramatically improved my life!*

Sincerely, J.B.

Dear Dr. Rath:

I'm a 51-year-old business executive. Because of my position I am consistently placed in high stress situations. My lifestyle and business responsibilities have caused me to be concerned about the potential of developing coronary artery disease.

Approximately two years ago I scheduled myself for a Coronary Artery Scan on an Ultrafast CT scanner. This new diagnostic technique allows the measurement of the small calcifications in the coronary arteries that are invariably associated with atherosclerotic plaques. The test was fast, painless, and involved no injections or any discomfort. The Coronary Artery Scan was performed at the South San Francisco HeartScan Clinic owned by Imatron, the company that developed the Ultrafast CT scanner.

*My Coronary Artery Scan two years ago and a second scan one year later showed the **beginnings of atherosclerosis in my coronary arteries.** A few months after my second scan was taken I was introduced to your vitamin-based cardiovascular health program. After eight months of following your program, I received an additional Coronary Artery Scan in order to evaluate the possible effect of your program on the calcium deposition in my coronary arteries. This most recent Coronary Artery Scan showed that the **calcifications in my coronary arteries had disappeared entirely. It was apparent to me that these deposits have been reversed, or eliminated, during your cardiovascular health program**.*

Because I was skeptical of the dramatic results, I scheduled a second follow-up Coronary Artery Scan at the HeartScan facility immediately after receiving the results. This follow-up scan confirmed the earlier results demonstrating no evidence of coronary artery calcification. I must also add that I have made no other significant changes in other aspects of my lifestyle during the past eight months - only your cardiovascular vitamin program. I want to offer you my sincere thanks.

Yours truly, S.L.M.

Dear Dr. Rath:

I am a 57 year old man and have lived a very active life. Two years ago I was diagnosed with **angina pectoris.** *The cardiologist prescribed a calcium antagonist and nitroglycerin tablets, as needed for pain. Dr. Rath,I was taking 8 to 10 nitroglycerin tablets weekly.*

Then I was introduced to your vitamin program and a fiber formula and within 6 weeks I no longer needed the nitroglycerin. I was not able to mow my yard with a push mower without stopping every 5 to 10 minutes and take a nitroglycerin tablet. **About a week ago I push mowed my entire yard, about three hours work. I did not stop at all and did not have any chest pain. I felt great.** *I have also lost about 10 pounds and my cholesterol level dropped from 274 to 191. My doctor says he is real pleased with my condition.*

I am indebted to you for a great change in my life. With your help I will be able to live a more fulfilling life for a longer time for a lot less money.

Thank you so very much. H.D.

Dear Dr. Rath:

I am an eighty-five year old woman. Ten years ago I was diagnosed with angina pectoris. **I was told by my doctor that two major arteries were 95% blocked.** *The doctor prescribed nitroglycerin tablets to relieve the painful condition induced by stress. I have been taking three nitroglycerin tablets a day for chest pains for 10 years.*

Last December I started on your cardiovascular vitamin program. After two months I was almost completely off nitroglycerin, *and now take a nitroglycerin tablet only occasionally.*

Sincerely, R.A.

Dear Dr. Rath:

In July I complained of chest pain and pain in my left arm. During a treadmill test of about 9 minutes, I had pain in my chest and numbness in my left arm. I was given nitroglycerine, and the pain went away immediately. The following day I was admitted to the hospital for an angiogram. The doctor also found that I had an overactive thyroid.

The results of the angiogram indicated that my left main (coronary) artery was 75% blocked and that I would need a double bypass. *The doctors didn't want to do the surgery until my thyroid condition was under control.*

In the meantime I started your cardiovascular vitamin program. I tripled the dosage, while continuing to take the doctor's prescribed medication. The heart surgeon called me for the open-heart surgery even though my thyroid condition was not yet under control. ***When the cardiologists set up a thallium treadmill test he was amazed about the results – they were normal, with no chest pain or shortness of breath. He told me that I could postpone the surgery indefinitely and to come back in six months.***

Just last week the doctor looked at my laboratory records and said: "This is amazing." He went across the hall to see the cardiologist to make sure the report was correct.
Thank you again, Dr. Rath. I think this is the beginning of the end of heart disease.

Sincerely,   J.K.

45

Dear Dr. Rath:

I was very excited about the possibility of improving heart function and reversing heart disease due to atherosclerosis after reading your books this past February. **I have familial hypercholesterolemia (high cholesterol) and had a myocardial infarction six years ago at age 40.**

I started following your cardiovascular vitamin program in February this year, along with a fiber formula. Within the first month, I started feeling less tired and was able to keep on going without exhaustion or angina. Within two months, the pain in my lower left leg due to poor circulation (atherosclerosis) disappeared. My heart feels like it's just on overdrive - just purring along - no longer pounding in my chest.

My annual physical in May was quite interesting. I never told my doctor I was doing anything different, but he shared with me that my ECG looked normal! **I asked my doctor about possibly lowering my heart medication (calcium antagonist, beta-blocker). He said that, based on my examination, he would take me off all this medicine** *if I lost 17 more pounds of weight. I had already lost 12 pounds since February, so I see losing 17 pounds just a matter of time.*

I have supplemented your vitamin program with additional vitamin C, L-proline, and L-lysine. I do not know if my atherosclerosis will ever be 100% reversed, but I do know that whatever progress your program has done for me so far has already improved my condition and has impacted my overall quality of life.

I will continue your cardiovascular health program the rest of my life, and recommend it to any concerned about their health.

I thank God for your research.

Sincerest regards, R.R.

Dear Dr. Rath:

I am a 57 year old male who had a heart attack on November 20, 1986. **I was told by my cardiologist that I had incurred a myocardial infarction** *of a small artery in the lower portion of my heart. It was determined that angioplasty or some other surgical procedure was not relevant or pertinent. The after effects were reduced energy and stamina, angina pectoris and other related symptoms typical to this condition. Since that time, I have been on a calcium antagonist medication. Follow up angioplasty procedures were performed in October 1987 and February 1993. Evidence of noticeable change in my condition was limited to some increase in the partial blockage in other major coronary arteries.*

I began following your cardiovascular vitamin program last October. This April another angioplasty was performed on me by a cardiologist who is highly respected and has many years of experience in this specialty area. He has performed several thousand of these procedures; however, he was amazed at what he observed in my case. **He found the previously blocked artery to have 25% to 30% blood flow and no advancement in the partial obstruction (blocking) of other arteries.** *His comment was, "Your arteries look great, I don't know what you are doing, but keep doing it."* **He further commented that this was only the second time he had observed an artery opening up that was previously blocked, without some surgical procedure.**

I have experienced remarkable improvement in my general health through a reduction in the incidence of angina, chest pressure, shortness of breath and increased energy and endurance. I truly believe your cardiovascular health program will extend my life and eliminate what appeared to the inevitable need for cardiac by-pass surgery some time in the future. Your program has dramatically improved my life and I am very grateful.

Sincerely, L.T.

> *Dear Dr. Rath:*
>
> *A friend of mine started on your vitamin program because of minor heart problems. I did not know, but he was also **scheduled for eye surgery because of blood vessel blockage.** He went into the hospital for surgery last week and the doctor looked into his eyes and couldn't believe what he saw. **His blockages had cleared and he no longer needed the surgery done!** Needless to say he has been telling everyone he knows about your cardiovascular health program.*
>
> *Sincerely, C.Z*

A growing number of health professionals around the world are recommending Dr. Rath's Vitamin Program for their patients as an adjunct therapy. They appreciate that finally a clinically tested natural health program is available. The benefits are evident as can be seen from the following patient letter to his doctor:

> *Dear Doctor:*
>
> *I can't wait to see you in six weeks. Since following Dr. Rath's Vitamin-Program. I have had no angina. This past month I have walked and climbed the rugged trails of the rain forest without so much as a twinge. And recently, I have walked the last two to eighteen holes of a golf course, something unheard of since my heart attack. In closing, I and my family are very pleased and would like to thank you.*
>
> *Sincerely, J.T.*

Clinical Studies Document Prevention of Cardiovascular Disease with Vitamins

The paramount importance of several components of Dr. Rath's Vitamin Program in the prevention of cardiovascular disease has also been documented in numerous clinical and epidemiological studies.

Dr. James Enstrom and his colleagues from the University of California at Los Angeles investigated vitamin intake of more than 11,000 Americans over ten years. This government-supported study showed that people who took at least 300 mg per day of vitamin C in their diet or in form of nutritional supplements, compared to 50 mg contained in an average American diet, could reduce their heart disease rate up to 50% in men and up to 40% in women. The same study showed that an increased intake of vitamin C was associated with an increased life expectancy of up to six years.

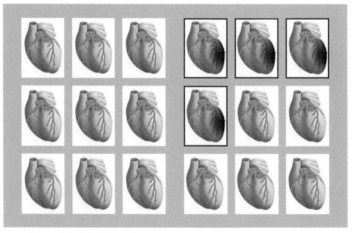

300 mg Vitamin C per Day: **Average Diet:**
Up to 50% Fewer Heart Attacks   **Increased Risk for Heart Attacks**

Vitamin C Cuts Risk for Heart Attacks in Half

49

The Canadian physician, Dr. G. C. Willis, showed that dietary vitamin C can reverse atherosclerosis. At the beginning of his study, he documented the atherosclerotic deposits in his patients by angiography (injection of a radioactive substance followed by X-ray pictures). After this documentation, half of the study patients received 1.5 grams of vitamin C per day. The other half of the patients received no additional vitamin C. The control analysis, on average, after 10 to 12 months, showed that in those patients who had received additional vitamin C, the atherosclerotic deposits had decreased in 30% of the cases. In contrast, no decrease in atherosclerotic deposits could be seen in those patients without vitamin C supplementation. The deposits in these patients either remained the same or had further increased. Amazingly, this important clinical study was conducted more than 40 years ago and was never followed up.

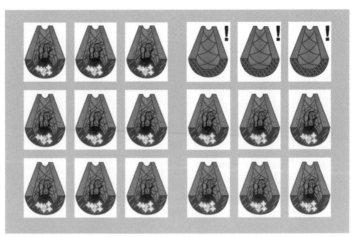

No Vitamin C Supplements: **1500 mg Vitamin C per Day:**
Coronary Deposits grow   **Halt and reversal in 30%**

Vitamin C Cuts Risk for Heart Attacks in Half

Europe: More Vitamins, Less Heart Disease

One of the largest studies about the importance of vitamins in the prevention of cardiovascular disease was conducted in Europe. It is a well-known fact that cardiovascular diseases are more frequent in Scandinavia and northern European countries as compared with Mediterranean countries. Professor Gey, from the University of Basel in Switzerland, compared the rate of cardiovascular disease in these countries to the blood levels

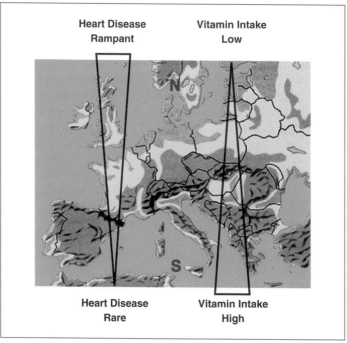

Heart Disease Rampant   **Vitamin Intake Low**

Heart Disease Rare   **Vitamin Intake High**

In Europe an inverse relationship between vitamin intake and the frequency of heart attacks and strokes has already been established. Cardiovascular diseases are much more common in northern European countries where vitamin intake is low.
Vice versa, people in Mediterranean countries enjoy a diet rich in vitamins and, consequently, cardiovascular disease is rare.

51

of vitamin C and beta carotene, as well as cholesterol. His findings were remarkable:

- People in northern European countries have the highest rate of cardiovascular disease and, on average, the lowest blood levels of vitamins.

- Southern European populations have the lowest cardiovascular risk and the highest vitamin blood levels.

- An optimum intake of vitamin C, E and A had a much greater impact on decreasing the risk for cardiovascular disease than lowering of cholesterol levels.

This study finally provides the scientific answer to the "French Phenomenon" and to the low rate of heart attacks in France, Greece, and other Mediterranean countries. The decisive factor for the low cardiovascular risk in these countries is an optimum intake of vitamins in the regular diets of these regions. Certain dietary preferences, such as the consumption of wine and olive oil, rich in bioflavonoids and vitamin E, seem to be of particular importance.

Vitamin E and Beta Carotene Also Decrease Your Cardiovascular Risk

Optimum dietary intake of vitamin E and beta-carotene also significantly reduce the cardiovascular risk. In several large-scale clinical studies, the importance of these vitamins for optimum cardiovascular health has been documented:

The Nurses' Health Study included more than 87,000 American nurses, ages 34 to 59. None of the study participants had any signs of cardiovascular disease at the beginning of the study. In 1993, a first result was published in the New England Journal of Medicine. It was shown that study participants taking more than 200 units of vitamin E per day could reduce their risk for heart attacks by 34%, compared to those receiving only 3 units, corresponding to the average daily intake of vitamin E in America.

The Health Professional Study included over 39,000 health professionals, ages 40 to 75. At the beginning of the study, none of the participants had any signs of cardiovascular disease or diabetes, or elevated blood cholesterol levels. The study showed that people taking 400 units of vitamin E per day could reduce their risk for heart attack by 40%, compared to those taking only 6 units of vitamin E per day. In the same study, an increased intake of beta-carotene was also shown to significantly decrease the cardiovascular risk.

The Physicians Health Study included over 22,000 physicians, ages 40 to 84. From this study in patients with existing cardiovascular disease, published by Dr. Hennekens in 1992, it was shown that in those patients, 50 mg of beta carotene per day could cut the risk for suffering a heart attack or stroke in half. The following table summarizes the results of these last clinical studies:

- Vitamin C Intake lowers cardiovascular risk by 50%, documented in 11,000 study participants over 10 years.

- Vitamin E supplementation lowers cardiovascular risk by one-third, documented in 87,000 study participants over 6 years.

- Beta carotene supplementation lowers cardiovascular risk over 30%, documented in more than 87,000 study participants over 6 years.

- No prescription drug has ever been shown to be as effective as these vitamins in preventing heart disease.

Vitamin C, vitamin E and beta-carotene are all essential components of Dr. Rath's Vitamin Program. Moreover, this program comprises the natural amino acids, lysine and proline, as well as the other natural substances that have been shown in numerous scientific studies to optimize cardiovascular health.

Cellular Medicine Program for Patients with Coronary Heart Disease

In addition to the basic vitamin program (page 23), patients with existing coronary heart disease or high risk for this condition are recommended to take the following cellular bio-energy factors in higher dosages or in addition.

- **Vitamin C:** protection and natural healing of the artery wall, reversal of plaques.

- **Vitamin E:** anti-oxidative protection.

- **Vitamin D:** optimizing of calcium metabolism, reversal of calcium deposits in artery walls.

- **Proline:** collagen production, stability of the artery wall, reversal of plaques.

- **Lysine:** collagen production, stability of the artery wall, reversal of plaques.

- **Folic acid:** protective function against increased homocystine levels together with Vitamin B6, Vitamin B12 and Biotin.

- **Biotin:** protective function against increased homocystine levels together with Vitamin B6, Vitamin B12 and folic acid.

- **Copper:** stability of the artery wall by improved cross-linking of collagen molecules.

- **Chondroitine sulfate:** stability of the artery wall as "cement" of the artery wall connective tissue.

- **N-Acetylglycosamine:** stability of the artery wall as "cement" of the artery wall connective tissue.

- **Pycnogenol:** bio-catalyst for improved vitamin C function, improved stability of the artery walls.

Background Information for Dr. Rath's Vitamin Program and Cardiovascular Disease

What Is Atherosclerosis?

The pictures on this page are cross-sections from coronary arteries of patients with coronary artery disease. These pictures provide a look inside these arteries through a microscope. The dark ring you notice is the original blood vessel wall as it would be found in a newborn baby. The gray area within this dark ring is atherosclerotic deposits which developed over many years.

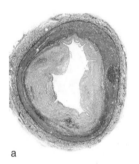 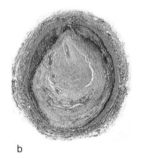

a   b

Picture A shows atherosclerotic deposits in coronary arteries, which reduce blood flow and impair oxygen and nutrient supply to millions of heart muscle cells. The coronary arteries of patients with angina pectoris typically look like this.

Picture B shows the coronary arteries of a patient who died from a heart attack. On top of the atherosclerotic deposits, a blood clot formed which completely interrupted the blood flow through this artery. This is called a heart attack. Millions of heart muscle cells die off, leaving the heart muscle permanently impaired or leading to the death of the patient.

It is important to understand that the atherosclerotic deposits in Picture A have developed over many years. In contrast, the additional blood clot in Picture B develops within minutes or seconds. Effective prevention of heart attacks has to start as early as possible by preventing atherosclerotic deposits. Atherosclerosis is not a disease of advanced age. Studies of soldiers killed in the Korean and Vietnam wars showed that up to 75% of the victims had already developed some form of atherosclerotic deposits at age 25 and younger. The picture below shows a coronary artery of a 25-year-old victim of a traffic accident. This coincidental finding shows how far atherosclerosis can advance in young adults – without causing any symptoms.

The main cause of atherosclerotic deposits is the biological weakness of the artery walls caused by chronic vitamin deficiency. The atherosclerotic deposits are the consequence of this chronic weakness; they develop as a compensatory stabilizing cast of Nature to strengthen these weakened blood vessel walls.

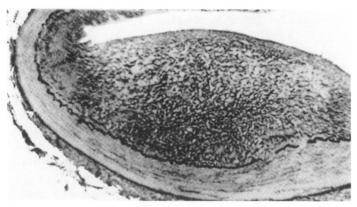

Cross section (magnified) of the coronary artery of a 25-year-old victim of a traffic accident. The atherosclerotic deposits had developed without the young man knowing or noticing anything.

Why Animals Don't Get Heart Attacks

According to the statistics of the World Health Organization, each year more than 12,000,000 people die from the conse-quences of heart attacks and strokes. Amazingly, while cardio-vascular disease has become one of the largest epidemics ever to haunt mankind, these very same heart attacks are essentially unknown in the animal world. The following paragraph from the renowned textbook of veterinary medicine by Professor H. A. Smith and T. C. Jones documents these facts:

> *"The fact remains, however, that in none of the domestic species, with the rarest of exceptions, do animals develop atherosclerotic disease of clinical significance. It appears that most of the pertinent pathological mechanisms ope-rate in animals and that atherosclerotic disease in them is not impossible; **it just does not occur.** If the reason for this could be found it might cast some very useful light on the human disease."*

These important observations were published in 1958. Now, almost four decades later, the puzzle of human cardiovascular disease has been solved. The solution to the puzzle of human cardiovascular disease is one of the great advances in medi-cine.

Here is the main reason why animals don't get heart attacks: With few exceptions, animals produce their own vitamin C in their bodies. The daily amounts of vitamin C produced vary between 1000 mg and 20,000 mg, when compared to the human body weight. Vitamin C is the cement of the artery wall, and optimum amounts of vitamin C stabilize the arteries. In contrast, we human beings cannot produce a single mole-cule of vitamin C ourselves. Our ancestors lost this ability gen-erations ago when an enzyme which was needed to convert sugar molecules (glucose) into vitamin C became defunct. This change in the molecules of inheritance (genes) of our ancestors had no immediate disadvantage since, for thousands of gener-

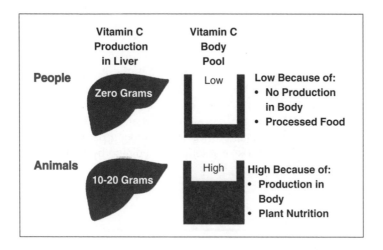

ations, they relied primarily on plant nutrition such as cereal, fruits and others, which provided the daily minimum of vitamins for them. Nutritional habits and dietary intake of vitamins changed considerably in this century. Today, most people do not receive sufficient amounts of vitamins in their diet. Still worse, food processing, long-term storage and overcooking destroy most vitamins in the food. The consequences are summarized in the picture above.

The single most important difference between the metabolism of human beings and most other living species is the dramatic difference in the body pool of vitamin C. The body reservoir of vitamin C in people is on average ten to 100 times lower than the vitamin C levels in animals.

How Does Vitamin C Prevent Atherosclerosis?

Vitamin C contributes in many different ways to the prevention of cardiovascular disease. It is an important antioxidant and it serves as a cofactor for many biochemical reactions in the body cells. The most important function of vitamin C in preventing heart attacks and strokes is its ability to increase the production of collagen, elastin, and other reinforcement mole-

59

Left: Cross section through an artery (magnified). Collagen and other connective tissue (white structures) provide basic stability to blood vessel walls.

Right: Individual collagen molecules under high magnification. Each of these fibers is stronger than an iron wire of comparable width.

cules in the body. These biological reinforcement rods constitute the connective tissue, about 50% of all proteins in our body. Collagen has the same structural stability function for our body as iron reinforcement rods have for a skyscraper building. Increased production of collagen means improved stability for the 60,000-mile-long walls of our arteries, veins, and capillaries.

The Scientific World Knows the Facts

The close connection between vitamin C deficiency and the instability of body tissue was established long ago. The following page is taken from the world-famous textbook on biochemistry by Professor Lubert Stryer of Stanford University. While the vitamin C-collagen-connection is firmly established, the paramount importance of this connection for heart disease has apparently been overlooked or neglected.

Defective Hydroxylation is one of the Biochemical Lesions in Scurvy

The importance of the hydroxylation of collagen becomes evident in scurvy. A vivid description of this disease was given by Jacques Cartier in 1536, when it afflicted his men as they were exploring the Saint Lawrence River:
"Some did lose all their strength and could not stand on their feet...others also had all their skins spotted with spots of blood of a purple color: then did it ascend up to their ankles, knees, thighs, shoulders, arms and necks. Their mouths became stinking, their gums so rotten, that all the flesh did fall off, even to the roots of the teeth which did also almost all fall out."

The means of preventing scurvy was succinctly stated by James Lind, a Scottish physician, in 1753: "Experience indeed sufficiently shows that as greens or fresh vegetables with ripe fruits, are the best remedies for it, so they prove the most effectual preservatives against it." Lind urged the inclusion of lemon juice in the diet of sailors. His advice was adopted by the British navy some 40 years later.

Scurvy is caused by a dietary deficiency of ascorbic acid (vitamin C). Primates and guinea pigs have lost the ability to synthesize ascorbic acid and so they must acquire it from their diets. Ascorbic acid, an effective reducing agent, maintains prolyl hydroxylase in an active form, probably by keeping its iron atom in the reduced ferrous state. Collagen synthesized in the absence of ascorbic acid is insufficiently hydroxylated and, hence, has a lower melting temperature. This abnormal collagen cannot properly form fibers and thus causes the skin lesions and blood vessel fragility that are so prominent in scurvy.

Atherosclerosis Is an Early Form of Scurvy

While these facts were known 250 years ago, they are still not applied in medicine today. The next figure summarizes the fact that the main cause of heart attacks and strokes is a scurvy-like condition of the artery wall.

Left column A: Optimum intake of vitamin C leads to an optimum production and function of collagen molecules. A stable blood vessel wall does not allow atherosclerotic deposits to develop. Optimum availability of vitamin C in their bodies is the main reason why animals don't get heart attacks.

Right column C: The right column of this figure summarizes the events in scurvy. Total depletion of the vitamin C body reserves, as they occurred in sailors of earlier centuries, leads to a gradual break-down of the body's connective tissue, including the vessel walls. Thousands of sailors died from hemorrhagic blood loss through leaky blood vessel walls within a few months.

Center column B: Atherosclerosis and cardiovascular disease are exactly between these two conditions. Our average diet contains enough vitamin C to prevent open scurvy, but not enough to guarantee stable reinforced artery walls. As a consequence, millions of tiny cracks and lesions develop along the artery walls. Subsequently, cholesterol, lipoproteins, and other blood risk factors enter the damaged artery walls in order to repair these lesions. With chronically low vitamin intake, however, this repair process continues over decades. Over many years this repair overcompensates or overshoots and atherosclerotic deposits develop. Deposits in the arteries of the heart eventually lead to heart attack; deposits in the arteries of the brain lead to stroke.

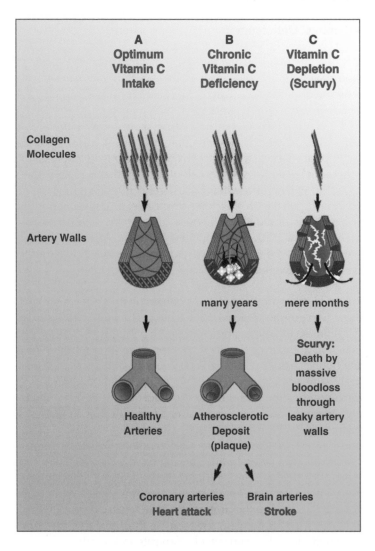

The Scurvy-Cardiovascular Disease Connection.
The connection between cardiovascular disease, vitamin C
deficiency, and scurvy is of such fundamental importance for our
health that this figure should become an essential part of the health
education in the schools of the world.

Vitamin C Deficiency Causes Atherosclerosis – The Proof

It is possible to prove that too low a dietary intake of vitamin C *alone,* without any other factors involved, directly causes atherosclerosis and cardiovascular disease. To prove this, we had to conduct an animal experiment with guinea pigs, exceptions in the animal world because they share with humans the inability to produce their own vitamin C. Two groups of guinea pigs received exactly the same daily amounts of cholesterol, fats, proteins, sugar, salt, and all other ingredients in their diet, with one exception – vitamin C. Group B received 60 mg of vitamin C per day in their diet, compared to the human body weight. This amount was chosen to meet the official recommended daily allowance for humans in the U.S. In contrast, group A received 5,000 mg of vitamin C per day compared to human body weight.

These pictures document the changes in the artery walls in these two groups after only five weeks. The first picture shows the differences in the arteries of the two groups.The vitamin C deficient animals of Group B developed atherosclerotic deposits (white areas), particularly in the areas close to the heart (right side of picture). The aortas of the animals in Group A remained healthy and did not show any deposits. The following pictures show the same artery walls examined under a microscope. The artery sections from animals with high vitamin C intake (A) show an intact cell barrier between the bloodstream and the artery wall. The almost parallel alignment of the collagen molecules in the artery wall makes stability visible. In contrast, the arteries of the vitamin C deficient animals (Group B) have lost the protection (defective barrier cell lining) and stability (fragmented collagen structure) of their arteries. For comparison, a picture of the coronary arteries from a patient with coronary artery disease was added (Picture C).

Note: In principle animal experiments should be kept to an absolute minimum. They are only justified when human lives can be saved with the knowledge that results from these experiments. This was the case with the experiment described, which brought millions of people the proof of the value of vitamin C for the prevention of heart attacks.

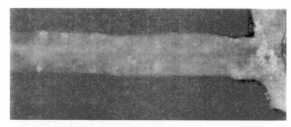

A
High
Vitamin C
Diet

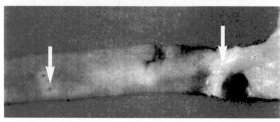

B
Low
Vitamin C
Diet

The main arteries (aortas) of animals on a high vitamin C diet (top picture) and on a low vitamin c diet (bottom picture). The white areas in the bottom picture are atherosclerotic deposits. These deposits are not the result of a high fat diet, but of the body's response to weak vitamin-deficient arteries.

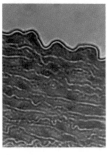
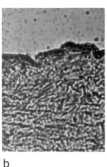

a   b   c

A look inside three different artery walls under the microscope:
A: Guinea pig on a high vitamin C diet.
B: Guinea pig on a low vitamin C diet.
C: Coronary artery of a patient who had died from a heart attack.

Note the similarity between picture B and C.

65

A New Understanding of the Nature of Heart Disease

The previous experiment underlines our modern definition of cardiovascular disease as a vitamin deficiency condition. This new understanding is summarized on the facing page:

1. **Lesions.** The main cause of cardiovascular disease is the instability and dysfunction of the blood vessel wall caused by chronic vitamin deficiency. This leads to millions of small lesions and cracks in the artery wall, particularly in the coronary arteries. The coronary arteries are mechanically the most stressed arteries because they are squeezed flat from the pumping action of the heart more than 100,000 times per day, similar to a garden hose which is stepped upon.

2. **Beginning Repair**. Repair of the artery walls then becomes necessary. Cholesterol and other repair factors are produced at an increased rate in the liver and are transported in the bloodstream to the artery walls, which they enter in order to mend and repair the damage. Because the coronary arteries sustain the most damage, they require the most intensive repair.

3. **Ongoing Repair**. With continued vitamin deficiency over many years, the repair process in the artery walls overcompensates. Atherosclerotic plaques form predominantly at those locations in the cardiovascular system with the most intensive repair: the coronary arteries. This is why infarctions occur primarily at this very same location and why the most frequent cardiovascular events are infarctions of the heart, not infarctions of the nose or ears.

1 Lesions in the Artery Wall

Atherosclerosis begins with millions of small cracks and lesions along the inside of the artery walls, as the result of chronic vitamin deficiency

2 Repair of Artery Wall

Repair factors from the blood stream (cholesterol, lipo-proteins etc.) as well as cell growth inside the artery walls are used by the body to stabilize and repair the weak arteries

3 Overcompensating Repair

With dietary vitamin deficiency continuing over many years, this repair inside the artery walls overcompensates or overshoots and atherosclerotic deposits develop

Atherosclerosis Develops in Three Steps

The Natural Reversal of Cardiovascular Disease

The basis for the reversal of atherosclerosis is the initiation of a healing process in the artery wall that has been weakened by chronic vitamin deficiency. Besides vitamin C, which stimulates production of collagen molecules, other constituents of Dr. Rath's Vitamin Program are also essential for this healing process. The figure on the adjacent page summarizes the protective functions of this essential nutrient program.

In the middle of the figure is the picture of a microscopic cross-section of the atherosclerotic deposit of a human coronary artery. The white area above the plaque represents the area where normally the blood flows. The lipoproteins (fat molecules) in the center of the deposits are stained black with a specific staining technique. Two of these lipoprotein (a) molecules (one lipoprotein (a) and one LDL molecule) among thousands of lipoprotein molecules in this plaque are schematically magnified. These lipoproteins have been deposited inside the artery wall for many years.

Around the core of the plaque a local "tumor" forms from muscle cells typical for the artery wall. This "muscle cell tumor"is another way by which the body stabilizes the vitamin-deprived artery wall. The deposition of lipoproteins from the bloodstream and the muscle cell tumor in the artery wall are the most important factors that determine the size of the plaque and, thereby, the growth of coronary heart disease. Any therapy that is able to reverse these two mechanisms of atherosclerosis must also reverse coronary heart disease itself. The ingredients of Dr. Rath's Vitamin Program synergistically affect both mechanisms in the following ways:

1   **Stability of the artery wall** through optimum collagen production. The collagen molecules in our body are proteins composed of amino acids. Collagen molecules differ from all other proteins in the body by the fact that they make particular use of the amino acids lysine and proline. We

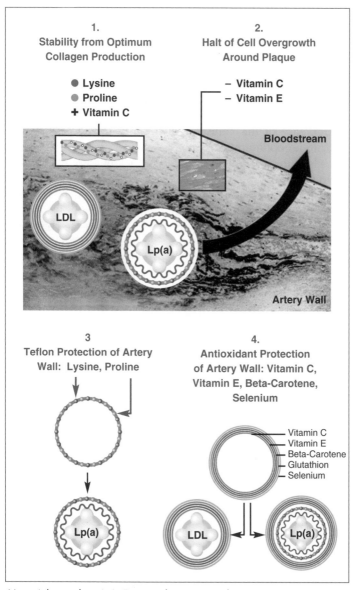

How Atherosclerosis Is Reversed in a Natural Way

already know that vitamin C stimulates the production of collagen in the cells of the artery wall. An optimum supply of lysine, proline, and vitamin C is a decisive factor for the optimum regeneration of the connective tissue in the artery walls and, therefore, for a natural healing of cardiovascular disease.

2 **Decrease of the "muscle cell tumor" in the artery wall.** With an optimum supply of essential nutrients, the muscle cells of the artery walls produce sufficient amounts of functional collagen, thereby guaranteeing optimum stability of the wall. In contrast, vitamin deficiency leads to the production of faulty and dysfunctional collagen molecules by the arterial muscle cells. Moreover, these muscle cells multiply themselves, forming the atherosclerotic "tumor." My colleague, Dr. Aleksandra Niedzwiecki and her colleagues investigated this mechanism in detail. They found that vitamin C, in particular, can inhibit the growth of the atherosclerotic "tumor." In the meantime, other studies have shown that vitamin E also has this effect.

3 **"Teflon" protection of the artery wall** and reversal of fatty deposits in the artery walls. Lipoproteins are the transport molecules by which cholesterol and other fat molecules circulate in the blood and are deposited in the artery walls. For many years, it has been thought that the primary transport molecule responsible for the deposition of fat in the artery walls is LDL (low-density lipoprotein, or "bad cholesterol"). Today, we know that the most dangerous fat transport molecules are not LDL molecules, but a variant, called lipoprotein (a). The letter (a) can stand for "adhesive" and characterizes an additional sticky protein which surrounds the LDL molecules. By means of this sticky protein the lipoprotein (a) molecules accumulate inside the artery walls. Thus, it is not the cholesterol or LDL-cholesterol level that determines the risk for cardiovascular disease, it is the amount of lipoprotein (a) molecules. In the next chapter I will discuss this new risk factor in detail.

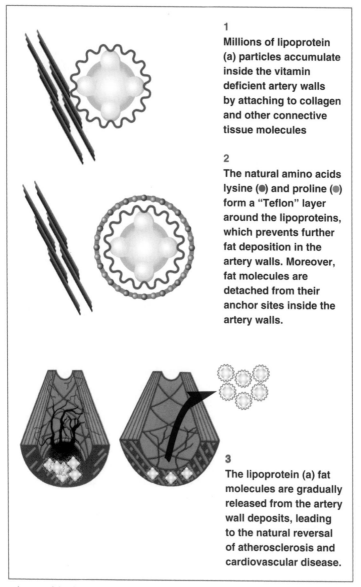

1

Millions of lipoprotein (a) particles accumulate inside the vitamin deficient artery walls by attaching to collagen and other connective tissue molecules

2

The natural amino acids lysine (●) and proline (●) form a "Teflon" layer around the lipoproteins, which prevents further fat deposition in the artery walls. Moreover, fat molecules are detached from their anchor sites inside the artery walls.

3

The lipoprotein (a) fat molecules are gradually released from the artery wall deposits, leading to the natural reversal of atherosclerosis and cardiovascular disease.

The world's first patented therapy for the natural reversal of atherosclerotic deposits

The primary therapeutic aim to prevent fatty deposits in the artery wall is therefore to neutralize the stickiness of the lipoprotein molecules and to prevent their attachment to the inside of the artery walls. This can be achieved by means of "Teflon" substances for the artery walls. The first generation of these "Teflon" agents has been identified. They are the natural amino acids lysine and proline. They form a protective layer around the lipoprotein (a) molecules, which has a twofold effect: preventing the deposition of more fat molecules in the artery wall and releasing lipoprotein molecules that had already been deposited inside the artery walls. Releasing fat molecules from the atherosclerotic deposits leads to a natural reversal of cardiovascular disease. Molecule by molecule is released from the atherosclerotic plaques into the bloodstream and transported to the liver, where these molecules are burned. It is important to understand that this is a natural process, and complications that frequently accompany angioplasty and other mechanical procedures do not occur.

4 **Antioxidant protection in the bloodstream and artery walls.** An additional mechanism accelerating the development of atherosclerosis, heart attacks and strokes, is biological oxidation. Free radicals, aggressive molecules occurring in cigarette smoke, car exhaust, and smog, damage the lipoproteins in the bloodstream and also the tissue of the artery walls. By doing so, they further extend the size of atherosclerotic plaques. Vitamin C, vitamin E, beta carotene, and other components of Dr. Rath's Vitamin Program belong to the strongest natural antioxidants, protecting the cardiovascular system from oxidative damage.

The reversal of fatty deposits in the artery wall is a process common in Nature. Bears and other hibernators, for example, use it regularly. During several months of winter sleep (hibernation) these animals do not eat, and therefore get no vitamins in their diet. Moreover, during hibernation the vitamin C production in their bodies decreases to a minimum. As a consequence, fat molecules and other factors from their blood are deposited in the artery walls and lead to a thickening of these walls. In spring, after these animals arise from hibernation, their vitamin supply increases dramatically from their diet and from their body's vitamin production. With this increased vitamin supply, the fatty deposits in the artery walls of these animals gradually reverse, and the artery walls retain their natural stability and function.

The solution to the puzzle of human cardiovascular disease is another striking example how a close look at Nature can help us to find solutions to human diseases.

Notes

High Cholesterol Levels and Other Secondary Risk Factors for Cardiovascular Disease

3

Dr. Rath's Vitamin program for Prevention and Adjunct Therapy

Cholesterol Is Only a Secondary Risk Factor

How Dr. Rath's Vitamin Program Can Help Patients With Elevated Cholesterol Levels

Clinical Studies with Components of Dr. Rath's Vitamin Program Known to Lower Risk Factors in Blood

Cholesterol Is Only a Secondary Risk Factor

Worldwide, hundreds of millions of people have elevated blood levels of cholesterol, triglycerides, LDL (low density lipoproteins), lipoprotein (a) and other risk factors in the blood. Contrary to what the pharmaceutical companies selling cholesterol-lowering drugs want to make you believe – there is nothing wrong with cholesterol levels of 220 or 240. Cholesterol is, at best, a "secondary" risk factor because the primary risk factor determining your cardiovascular risk is the weakness and instability of your blood vessel walls. Elevated blood levels of cholesterol and other blood risk factors are not the cause of cardiovascular diseases, but already the consequence of developing disease.

Conventional medicine is limited to treating the symptoms of secondary risk factors. Drugs blocking the synthesis of cholesterol and other lipid-lowering agents are now being prescribed to millions of people These drugs are known to cause cancer and other severe side effects and you should avoid them whenever you can.

Again, the reasons for elevated cholesterol levels are only partially understood by conventional medicine. Inherited disorders (genetic risk) and a high fat diet (dietary risk) are the two main reasons given in the textbooks of medicine. The most important reason is completely missing: a chronic deficiency of vitamins and other essential nutrients.

Modern Cellular Medicine provides a new understanding about the factors causing high blood levels of cholesterol and other secondary risk factors, as well as their natural prevention. Cholesterol, triglycerides, low density lipoproteins (LDL), lipoprotein (a) and other metabolic products are ideal repair factors, and their blood levels increase in response to a weakening of the artery walls. A chronic weakness of the blood vessel walls increases the demand and, thereby, the production rate of these repair molecules in the liver. An increased pro-

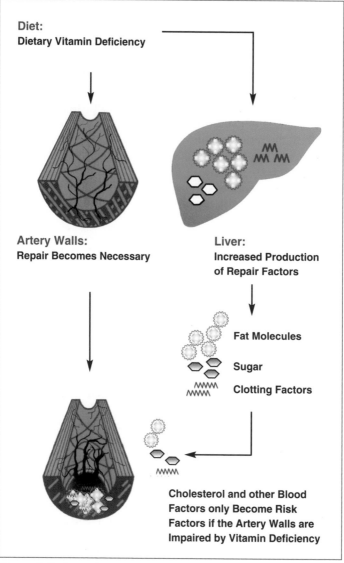

Diet:
Dietary Vitamin Deficiency

Artery Walls:
Repair Becomes Necessary

Liver:
**Increased Production
of Repair Factors**

Fat Molecules

Sugar

Clotting Factors

**Cholesterol and other Blood
Factors only Become Risk
Factors if the Artery Walls are
Impaired by Vitamin Deficiency**

*Elevated Cholesterol Levels Are Not the Cause, But Already the
Consequence of Cardiovascular Disease*

duction of cholesterol and other repair factors in the liver increases the levels of these molecules in the bloodstream and, over time, renders them risk factors for cardiovascular disease. Thus, the primary measure for lowering cholesterol and other secondary risk factors in the bloodstream is to stabilize the artery walls and thereby decrease the metabolic demand for increased production of these risk factors inside the body itself. Therefore, it is not surprising that Dr. Rath's Vitamin Program stabilizes the artery walls, and also, in parallel, helps to decrease blood levels of cholesterol and other risk factors naturally.

Cellular Medicine now also helps to expand our understanding about the different risk factors determining the individual cardiovascular risk:

Risk Factor	Can You Decrease Risk?
• Vitamin Deficiency	Yes
• Diet and Lifestyle	Yes
• Inherited Disorders	Yes
For details see chapters 4 and 5 of this book.	

Scientific research and clinical studies have already documented the particular value of vitamin C, vitamin B3 (nicotinate), vitamin B5 (pantothenate), vitamin E, carnitine, as well as other components of Dr. Rath's Vitamin Program for the lowering of elevated cholesterol levels and other secondary risk factors in the blood.

Dr. Rath's Vitamin Program comprises a selection of vitamins and other essential nutrients helping to normalize elevated levels of secondary risk factors. These essential nutrients lower the production rate of cholesterol and other repair molecules in the liver and, at the same time, contribute to the repair of the artery walls.

My recommendations for patients with elevated cholesterol and other secondary risk factors. Cholesterol-lowering without first stabilizing the artery walls is an insufficient and ill-fated cardiovascular therapy. Start as early as possible to increase the stability of your artery walls by using Dr. Rath's Vitamin Program. As a consequence, blood levels of cholesterol and other risk factors generally normalize. If you are on cholesterol or lipid lowering medication, I encourage you to discontinue this medication as soon as possible. All currently prescribed cholesterol-lowering drugs can cause cancer. Read about the "Cholesterol Fallacy" later in this chapter.

What You Should Do:

1   Clear your mind from the brainwash that cholesterol causes heart disease.

2   Stabilize your artery walls with Dr. Rath's Vitamin Program.

3   Eat more cereal, vegetables and other fiber-rich nutrition to "flush out"abundant cholesterol from your body naturally.

4   Stop taking cholesterol-lowering medication!

How Dr. Rath's Vitamin Program Can Help Patients With Elevated Cholesterol Levels

The following section documents letters from patients with cholesterol and other lipid disorders who have been helped with Dr. Rath's Vitamin Program. Please share this important information with friends and colleagues, thereby enabling them to lower their cholesterol levels in a natural way and stop taking harmful cholesterol medication.

Dear Dr. Rath,

*Heart disease is hereditary within my family and my father had his first heart attack in his early thirties. I had my cholesterol checked at age 19 only to find out that **I had a cholesterol level of 392 mg/dl**. My physician did not want to place me on medication at that time, so I just watched my diet and increased my exercise. Well, as time passed, my cholesterol remained elevated and my physician felt medication was necessary. I refused to begin medication and continued with diet and exercise.*

*At age 26 I had my cholesterol tested before I began your vitamin program, and my lab test showed a reading of 384. I immediately began following your program, including a fiber drink, and my level dropped 120 points within a 6-10 week period. **Over a four-month period, my LDL went from 308 down to 205.** Now there is a program, which I personally follow and continue to have positive results with.*

I recommend it to my family and friends.

Sincerely,   C.C.

Dear Dr. Rath,

I had started taking a fiber product in February of 1994. **My cholesterol continued to climb from 280 to over 320 until May of
1994, when I began to follow your cardiovascular vitamin program.**

**My cholesterol has dropped to 180, my ratio of HDL to LDL is
normal as is my triglyceride level.** *Most important, however, my
lipoprotein (a) dropped from 15 to 1! I will continue your program forever. Thank you, Dr. Rath, for your work with natural
products as a means to decreasing the risk of heart disease.*

With much gratitude,
M.R.

Dear Dr. Rath,

*I am 45 years old and since December last year I have been on
your program of essential nutrients and I also take a fiber formula.*
**Last April my cholesterol level was 259. This April, after only 4
months on this program, my cholesterol dropped to 175!**

*Dr. Rath, I truly want to thank you for helping me to be healthier
and able to live a much fuller life.*

Sincerely,
M.W.

In most people who start Dr. Rath's Vitamin Program the blood levels of cholesterol and other risk factors in the blood decrease relatively soon. We already know the reason for this effect: this essential nutrient program reduces the production rate of cholesterol and other secondary risk factors in the liver and thereby must lead to lower blood levels of this risk factor.

Interestingly, some patients report an intermittent rise of cholesterol levels when they start taking vitamins. Because the rise of blood cholesterol levels is not the result of an increased cholesterol production, it has to come from other sources primarily the atherosclerotic deposits in the artery walls. This important mechanism was first described by Dr. Constance Spittle in the medical journal *The Lancet* in 1972. She reported that vitamin supplementation in patients with existing cardiovascular disease frequently leads to a temporary increase of cholesterol levels in the blood. In contrast, the cholesterol levels of healthy test persons did not rise with vitamin supplementation.

The temporary rise of cholesterol is an additional sign of the healing process of the artery walls and the decrease of the fatty deposits. The mechanism described here is, of course, not only valid for cholesterol but also for triglycerides, LDL, lipoprotein (a), and other secondary risk factors which have accumulated over decades inside the artery walls and are now slowly released into the bloodstream.

My recommendation:

should your cholesterol levels rise when you start following this program, it signifies the reversal of existing deposits. You should continue the vitamin program until, after several months, the blood level of cholesterol decreases below the initial values. A diet high in soluble fiber (e.g. in oat bran and other cereals) can further decrease cholesterol and other secondary risk factors in the blood.

The following letter documents the rise and subsequent decrease of cholesterol on Dr. Rath's Vitamin Program:

Dear Dr. Rath,

I began taking a fiber formula two years ago in September. My total cholesterol was around 177 at that time. Within 90 days, I lost 20 pounds and my total cholesterol dropped to 154.

In November last year I started with your vitamin program. An insurance physical that was done in February this year showed a total cholesterol (CHOL) level of 191, triglycerides 244. LDL/HDL ratio of 4.09, CHOL/HDL ratio of 6.8, all of which were elevated. Again, note that this was in February.

A cholesterol screening was done in March and again in June. Both showed a total cholesterol level of 134. **A lipid profile that was done in July showed total cholesterol level 135, triglycerides 180. LDL/HDL ratio of 1.47., and CHOL/LDL ratio down to 3.16 from 6.8.**

Your cardiovascular health program is working!

Sincerely,
L.M.

Clinical Studies with Components of Dr. Rath's Vitamin Program Known to Lower Risk Factors in Blood

The effect of vitamin C on the blood levels of cholesterol and other blood fats has been documented in numerous clinical studies. More than 40 of these studies have been evaluated by Dr. Hemilä from the University of Helsinki, Finland. In patients with high initial cholesterol values (above 270 mg per deciliter) vitamin C supplementation has been able to decrease cholesterol levels up to 20%. In contrast, patients with low and medium initial values of cholesterol show only a slight choles-terol-lowering effect, or the levels stay the same.

In a study sponsored by the American Heart Association, Dr. Sokolov showed that two to three grams of vitamin C per day could lower triglycerides blood levels on average by 50% to 70%. It was shown that vitamin C increased the production of enzymes (lipases) able to degrade triglycerides and lower triglyceride levels.

Dr. Jacques and his colleagues could show that people taking 300 mg of Vitamin C per day and more also had much higher HDL blood levels than people taking less than 120 mg per day. This is particularly important since HDL (high-density lipopro-teins) are those fat-transporting molecules that can pick up cholesterol and other fats from the artery walls and carry it back to the liver for removal. This is yet another way how vita-min C can help reduce atherosclerotic deposits and thereby reverse cardiovascular disease. Dr. Hermann and his col-leagues reported that vitamin E supplementation also increases HDL blood levels.

Further clinical studies show that other components of Dr. Rath's Vitamin Program work synergistically with vitamin C in lowering cholesterol and other blood fats. These components include vitamin B3 (nicotinic acid), vitamin B5 (pantothenate), vitamin E, carnitine, and other essential nutrients. This synergistic effect is an important advantage compared to megadose intake of individual vitamins.

Clinical Study with	Reference
Vitamin C	Ginter, Harwood, Hemilä
Vitamin B-3	Altschul, Carlson, Guraker
Vitamin B-5	Avogaro, Cherchi, Gaddi
Vitamin E	Beamish, Hermann
Carnitine	Opie

Lipoprotein (a) – A Secondary Risk Factor – Ten Times More Dangerous Than Cholesterol

On the following pages I would like to introduce you to a particularly important secondary risk factor, lipoprotein (a). The genuine function of lipoprotein (a) is very useful; it fulfills a variety of repair functions, for example, during wound healing. However, if the artery wall is destabilized by a long- term vitamin deficiency, lipoprotein (a) turns into a risk factor ten times more dangerous than cholesterol. Let's have a closer look at how lipoprotein (a) molecules differ from other fat molecules.

Cholesterol and triglycerides do not swim in the blood like fat swims in the soup. Thousands of cholesterol molecules are packed together with other fat molecules in tiny round globules called lipoproteins. Millions of these fat-transporting vehicles circulate in our body at any given time. The best known among these lipoproteins are high-density lipoproteins (HDL, or "good cholesterol") and low-density lipoproteins (LDL, or "bad cholesterol").

LDL-cholesterol. Most of the cholesterol molecules in the blood are transported in millions of LDL particles. By carrying cholesterol and other fat molecules to our body cells, LDL is a very useful transport vehicle to supply nutrients to these cells.

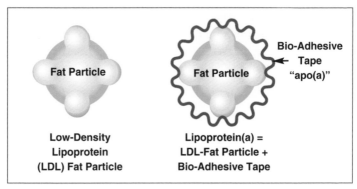

Comparison Between LDL and Lipoprotein(a)

LDL has been named the "bad cholesterol" because, until recently, researchers believed that it is LDL that is primarily responsible for the fatty deposits in the artery walls. This understanding is now out of date.

Lipoprotein (a) is an LDL particle with an additional adhesive protein surrounding it. This biological adhesive tape is named apoprotein (a), or brief, apo (a). The letter (a) could in fact

---

What Does Medicine Today Know About Lipoprotein (a)?

- Lipoprotein (a), not LDL, is the most important fat particle responsible for the deposition of cholesterol and other fats in the artery walls.
- Because of its sticky properties, lipoprotein (a) is one of the most effective repair molecules in the artery wall and, with ongoing vitamin deficiency, becomes one of the most dangerous risk factors for atherosclerosis and cardiovascular disease.
- A reevaluation of the Framingham Heart Study, the largest cardiovascular risk factor study ever conducted, showed that lipoprotein (a) is a ten-fold greater risk factor for heart disease than cholesterol or LDL-cholesterol.

---

stand for "adhesive." The adhesive apo (a) makes the lipoprotein (a) fat globule one of the stickiest particles in our body.

**In a Vitamin-Deficient Body, Lipoprotein (a) Becomes the
Most Important Secondary Risk Factor for:**

- Coronary Heart Disease and Heart Attacks
- Cerebrovascular Disease and Strokes
- Restenosis (Clogging) after Coronary Angioplasty
- Clogging of Bypass Grafts after Coronary Bypass Surgery

Together with my colleagues at Hamburg University, I conducted the most comprehensive studies on lipoprotein (a) in
the artery wall. These studies showed that the atherosclerotic
lesions in human arteries are largely composed of lipoprotein
(a) rather than LDL molecules. Moreover, the size of the atherosclerotic lesions paralleled the amount of lipoprotein (a) particles deposited in the arteries. In the meantime, these findings
have been confirmed in a series of further clinical studies.

Lipoprotein (a) blood levels vary greatly between one individual and another. What do we know about the factors influenc-
ing the lipoprotein (a) levels in your blood? Lipoprotein (a) levels are primarily determined by inheritance. Special diets do
not influence lipoprotein (a) blood levels. Moreover, none of
the presently available lipid-lowering prescription drugs lower
lipoprotein (a) blood concentrations. The only substances that
have thus far been shown to lower lipoprotein (a) levels are vitamins. Professor Carlson could show that two to four grams of
vitamin B3 (nicotinic acid) a day could lower lipoprotein (a)
levels up to 36%. Because high levels of nicotinic acid can
cause skin rash, you are well advised to increase the daily
intake of nicotinic acid slowly. Our own research showed that
vitamin C alone or in combination with lower dosages of nicotinic acid may also have a decreasing effect on the production
of lipoproteins and thereby on lowering lipoprotein blood levels. Together with the "Teflon" agents lysine and proline, these

two vitamins can considerably decrease the cardiovascular risk associated with lipoprotein (a) levels.

Therapeutic Approaches to Reduce the Risk from Lipoprotein (a)

1 Lowering of Lipoprotein (a) Blood Levels
   – Vitamin B3 (Nicotinate)
   – Vitamin C

2 Decreasing Stickiness of Lipoprotein(a)
   – Lysine
   – Proline

Lipoprotein (a) is a particularly interesting molecule because of its inverse relationship to vitamin C. The following discovery triggered my interest in vitamin research: lipoprotein (a) molecules are primarily found in humans and a few animal species unable to produce vitamin C. In contrast, animals able to produce optimum amounts of vitamin C do not need lipoprotein (a) in any significant amount. Lipoprotein (a) molecules apparently compensates for many properties of vitamin C such as wound healing and blood vessel repair. In 1990 I published the details of this important discovery in the *Proceedings of the National Academy of Sciences* and invited Linus Pauling as co-author for this publication.

The Cholesterol – Heart Disease Fallacy

While reading this section you may have asked yourself the question: "But what about cholesterol? Are those reports about cholesterol only media hype?" Unfortunately, this is the case. Here are some of the sobering facts:

The leading medical speculation about the origin of cardiovascular disease is as follows: high levels of cholesterol and risk factors in the blood circulation would damage the blood vessel walls and lead to atherosclerotic deposits. According to this hypothesis, lowering of cholesterol is the primary measure to prevent cardiovascular disease. Tens of millions of people worldwide are currently swallowing cholesterol-lowering drugs in the expectation of helping fight cardiovascular diseases. The marketing propaganda behind these cholesterol-lowering drugs is worthy of a close look:

In the 70's the World Health Organization (WHO) conducted an international study to answer the question whether cholesterol-lowering drugs can decrease the risk for heart attacks. Thousands of study participants received the cholesterol-lowering drug Clofibrate. This study could not be completed because those people who took the cholesterol-lowering drug experienced too many side effects. Thus, in the interest of the health and lives of the study participants, this cholesterol-lowering drug study had to be called off.

In the early 80's a large-scale study in over 3,800 American men made headline news. In this study it was tested whether the cholesterol-lowering drug Cholestyramine can lower the risk for heart attacks. One study group took up to 24 grams (24,000 milligrams) of Cholestyramine every day over several years. The control group of this study took the same amount of placeboes (ineffective control substance). The result of this study was that in the cholesterol-lowering drug group the same number of people died as in the control group. Particularly frequent among those patients taking this cholesterol-lowering drug were accidents and suicides. Irrespective of these facts, those interested in marketing the drug decided to sell this study as a success. The fact that in the drug group there were slightly fewer incidences of heart attacks was marketed as a confirmation of the cholesterol-heart attack-hypothesis. Hardly anyone bothered with the actual death figures of this study.

In the late 80's a new group of cholesterol-lowering drugs was introduced which was shown to decrease the production of cholesterol in the body. Soon thereafter it was determined that these drugs not only lower the production of cholesterol in the

89

body, but also the manufacturing of other essential substances in the body, for example, ubiquinone (Coenzyme Q-10). Professor Karl Folkers, from the University of Texas in Austin, rang the alarm bells in the Proceedings of the National Academy of Science. Professor Folkers reported that patients with existing heart failure taking these new cholesterol-lowering drugs could experience life-threatening deterioration of their heart functions.

A giant blow for the cholesterol-lowering drug industry came on January 6, 1996. On this day the Journal of the American Medical Association published an article entitled "Carcinogenicity of Cholesterol-lowering Drugs." Dr. Newman and Dr. Hulley from San Francisco University Medical School showed that most of the cholesterol-lowering drugs on the market are known to cause cancer in test animals at levels currently prescribed to hundreds of thousands of people. The results from this article were so alarming that the authors raised the legitimate question: "How could it be that the regulatory agency, the U.S. Food and Drug Administration, (FDA), allowed these drugs to be sold to millions of people?" The answer is: "The pharmaceutical companies manufacturing these drugs down played the importance of these side effects and thereby removed any obstacles for their approval."

The publication of my popular science book in 1993 explained for the first time that animals don't get heart attacks because they produce enough vitamin C - not because they have low cholesterol levels. Heart attacks are the primary result of vitamin deficiencies - not of elevated cholesterol. It was immediately clear that cholesterol-lowering drugs, beta-blockers, calcium antagonists and many other pharmaceuticals would eventually be replaced by essential nutrients in eliminating cardiovascular diseases. The time this would take would be dependent on one factor only: How fast can the information about the connection between scurvy and cardiovascular disease be spread. The manufacturers of cardiovascular drugs knew that they will loose an annual drug market of over $100

billion dollars. This multi-billion dollar drug market will collapse once millions of people learn that vitamins and other
essential nutrients are the answer to the cardiovascular epidemic.

This is the background why the pharmaceutical industry is
spending hundreds of millions of dollars advertising drugs that
are known to cause cancer.

Why Bears Are Not Extinct

If anyone among my readers still thinks that cholesterol may cause heart attacks, I would like to share the following facts: Bears and millions of other hibernating animals have average cholesterol levels of over 400 milligrams per deciliter. If cholesterol were, indeed, the culprit causing heart attacks and strokes, bears and millions of other hibernating animals would have long been extinct from heart attacks. The reason why bears are still among us is simple: they produce high amounts of vitamin C in their bodies, stabilize their artery walls and don't bother about cholesterol.

The fact that bears are not extinct proves:
1 Elevated cholesterol blood levels are not the primary cause of atherosclerosis, heart attacks and strokes.
2 Achieving and maintaining stability of the artery walls through optimum vitamin supply is more important than lowering cholesterol and other risk factors in the blood stream.
3 Cholesterol and other repair factors in the blood stream can only become risk factors if the artery walls are weakened by chronic vitamin deficiency.

Cellular Medicine Formula for Patients with High Cholesterol and Other Metabolic Disorders

In addition to the basic vitamin program (page 18-19), patients with elevated cholesterol levels and other metabolic disorders are recommended to take the following cellular bio-energy factors in higher dosages:

- **Vitamin C:** protection and natural healing of the artery walls, lowering increased production of cholesterol and other secondary risk factors in the liver and elevated blood levels of these secondary risk factors.

- **Vitamin E:** anti-oxidant protection for blood fats and millions of body cells.

- **Vitamin B1:** optimizing cellular metabolism, particularly delivery of bio-energy.

- **Vitamin B2:** optimizing cellular metabolism, particularly delivery of bio-energy.

- **Vitamin B3:** lowering elevated production of cholesterol and lipoproteins in the liver.

- **Vitamin B5:** structural component of the central metabolic molecule of cells (co-enzyme A), optimized metabolic burning of fat molecules.

- **Vitamin B6, biotin and folic acid:** counteracting increased levels of the risk factor *homocystine,* optimizing metabolism of cells.

- **Carnitine:** optimizing cellular metabolism of fats, lowering of triglyceride levels.

Notes

High Blood Pressure

4

Dr. Rath's Vitamin program for Prevention and Adjunct Therapy

The Facts About High Blood Pressure

How Patients With High Blood Pressure Benefit from Dr. Rath's Vitamin Program

Further Scientific Information Related to High Blood Pressure and Dr. Rath's Vitamin Program

Further Clinical Studies With Vitamins and High Blood Pressure

The Facts About High Blood Pressure

Worldwide several hundred million people suffer from high blood pressure conditions. Of all cardiovascular conditions, this is the single largest epidemic. The epidemic spread of this disease is largely due to the fact that, until now, the causes for high blood pressure have been insufficiently or not at all understood.

Conventional medicine concedes that the causes of high blood pressure are unknown in over 90% of patients. The frequent medical diagnosis, "essential hypertension" was established to describe the high blood pressure conditions in which the causes remain unknown. Accordingly, conventional medicine is confined to treating the symptoms of this disease. Beta-blockers, diuretics and other high blood pressure medications target the symptoms of high blood pressure, but not its underlying cause.

Modern Cellular Medicine provides a breakthrough in our understanding of the causes, prevention and adjunct therapy of high blood pressure conditions. The main cause of high blood pressure is a chronic deficiency of essential nutrients in millions of artery wall cells. Among other functions, these cells are responsible for the production of "relaxing factors" which decrease vascular wall tension and keep the blood pressure in a normal range. The natural amino acids arginine, vitamin C and other components of Dr. Rath's Vitamin Program contribute to optimum availability of these artery wall relaxing factors. In contrast, chronic deficiency of these essential nutrients can result in spasms and thickening of the blood vessel walls, and can eventually elevate blood pressure.

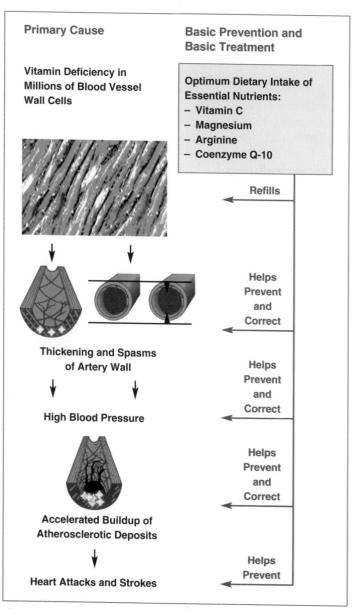

Primary Cause

Basic Prevention and Basic Treatment

Vitamin Deficiency in Millions of Blood Vessel Wall Cells

Optimum Dietary Intake of Essential Nutrients:
– **Vitamin C**
– **Magnesium**
– **Arginine**
– **Coenzyme Q-10**

Refills

Thickening and Spasms of Artery Wall

Helps Prevent and Correct

High Blood Pressure

Helps Prevent and Correct

Helps Prevent and Correct

Accelerated Buildup of Atherosclerotic Deposits

Helps Prevent and Correct

Heart Attacks and Strokes

Helps Prevent

Causes, Prevention and Adjunct Treatment of High Blood Pressure

Scientific research and clinical studies have already documented the value of vitamin C, magnesium, coenzyme Q-10, arginine, and other essential nutrients in helping to normalize high blood pressure conditions. Dr. Rath's Vitamin Program comprises selected essential nutrients that are needed for optimum functioning of vascular wall cells, and thereby contribute to preventing high blood pressure conditions and help to reverse existing high blood pressure disease.

My recommendations for high blood pressure patients: start immediately with this vitamin program and inform your doctor about it. Follow this program in addition to your regular medication. Do not stop or change your regular medication without consulting your doctor.

Prevention is better than treatment. The success of Dr. Rath's Vitamin Program in patients with high blood pressure conditions is based on the fact that millions of artery wall cells are supplied with cell fuel for optimum function. A natural cardiovascular program that contributes to correcting high blood pressure conditions is, of course, your best choice to prevent the development of high blood pressure conditions in the first place.

How Patients With High Blood Pressure Benefit from Dr. Rath's Vitamin Program

The following section documents a selection of letters from patients with high blood pressure conditions who are following Dr. Rath's Vitamin Program. With the help of this book, millions of high blood pressure patients around the world can now also take advantage of this natural medical breakthrough.

Dear Dr. Rath:

*About 8 weeks ago I was introduced to a fiber product for the reduction of my cholesterol, which had reached 260 in spite of efforts to get it down. After being on that product about 2 and a half weeks, I realized that my blood pressure was going up. **I am on blood pressure medication for essential hypertension since my teen years.** I supposed that it was due to the energy I was feeling from the fiber formula.*

*Then I heard about your essential nutrient program and that it had lowered blood pressure. I immediately started on your program. **Within two weeks my blood pressure had gone from 145/150 over 90/96 to 130/82 - sometimes a bit higher if I am really busy!** I noticed a lessening of a feeling of chest pressure also, and I could breathe deeper.*

Sincerely,
S.S.

Dear Dr. Rath:

I am a 53 year old man and my blood pressure was being con-trolled by blood pressure medication. **I had been taking blood pressure medication of various types for 10 years.**

After 4 months on your cardiovascular vitamin program, I went off all blood pressure medication, while my blood pressure was checked every two weeks. My blood pressure has now been nor-mal for 6 weeks, only with your cardiovascular health program. I had noticed some angina prior to this program, and those symp-toms have also been eliminated.

Sincerely,
J.L

Dear Dr. Rath,

I have been following your cardiovascular vitamin program for five months. In the meantime my doctor reduced my blood pres-sure medication by half so I can honestly say I'm now taking half the medication than five months ago. I am maintaining blood pressure average of 120/78. Thrilled? You'd better believe it! Next goal: no medication at all. Thank you again.

Sincerely,
L.M.

Dear Dr. Rath,

I am a 52-year old male with a high blood pressure problem that spans 25 years. I've been through six different physicians and I've lost count of the different blood pressure medications that have been prescribed for me. The best that any doctor was able to reduce my blood pressure to was an average of 135/95 for the last five or six years with a combination of prescription medication.

*I began following your vitamin program last December. My blood pressure dropped to an average of 124/82 by the first week of January, along with a greater feeling of energy and well-being. That occurred despite no change in diet or lifestyle. **My doctor reduced one of my blood pressure medications by half and my blood pressure still dropped over the next few months to an average of 122/80.***

The third week of May last year, it dropped to 120/64. So far, that level seems to be the start of a trend, so I'll have to visit my doctor again for a further reduction in medication.
I am now absolutely convinced that your cardiovascular program did really help to lower my blood pressure and all I can say is a big 'Thank You'.

Sincerely,
L.M.

Further Scientific Information Related to High Blood Pressure and Dr. Rath's Vitamin Program

This page summarizes in more detail the mechanisms by which Dr. Rath's Vitamin Program helps patients to normalize high blood pressure conditions. The following therapeutic mechanisms have been identified for one or more of the ingredients of this vitamin program:

Arginine, the natural amino acid, splits off an artery wall "relaxing factor," a small molecule called nitric oxide. Nitric oxide increases the elasticity of the artery walls, and thereby helps to normalize high blood pressure.

Vitamin C increases the production of prostacycline, a small molecule which not only relaxes the blood vessel walls, but also keeps the blood viscosity at optimum levels.

Magnesium, Nature's calcium antagonist, is essential for an optimum mineral balance in the blood vessel wall cells. Optimum mineral balance is a precondition for relaxation of the artery walls.

Lysine and proline help protect the artery walls and prevent the development of atherosclerotic deposits. This important mechanism was discussed in the first chapters of this book in detail. Since atherosclerosis is intertwined with high blood pressure, these ingredients are also essential to prevent and correct this health condition.

All these components are part of Dr. Rath's Vitamin Program.

Further Clinical Studies With Vitamins and High Blood Pressure

Various clinical studies show that different components of Dr. Rath's Vitamin Program are able to lower high blood pressure conditions. The following table summarizes some of the most important studies:

Components of Dr. Rath's Vitamin Program	Blood Pressure-Lowering	Reference
Vitamin C	5% to 10%	McCarron
Coenzyme Q-10	10% to 15%	Digiesi
Magnesium	10% to 15%	Turlapaty, Widman
Arginine	more than 10%	Korbut

It is important to note that in all these studies the natural components helped to normalize the blood pressure, but did not cause a too-low blood pressure situation. This is another advantage compared to conventional medication, where over-dosing frequently leads to decreased blood circulation, dizziness, and other health problems.

Cellular Medicine Program for Patients with High Blood Pressure

In addition to the basic vitamin program (page 18-19), patients with elevated blood pressure are recommended to take the following bio-energy cell factors in higher dosages:

- **Vitamin C:** decreased tension of the artery wall, increased supply of relaxing factors, lowering of elevated blood pressure.

- **Vitamin E:** anti-oxidant protection, protection of cell membranes and blood components.

- **Arginine:** improved production of "relaxing factors", decreased tension of the artery walls, lowering of elevated blood pressure.

- **Magnesium:** optimizing cellular metabolism of minerals, decreased tension of the blood vessel walls, lowering of high blood pressure.

- **Calcium:** optimizing mineral metabolism, decreased tension of the artery walls, lowering of high blood pressure.

- **Bioflavonoids:** catalysts, which among others, improve the efficacy of vitamin C.

Heart Failure

5

Dr. Rath's Vitamin program for Prevention and Adjunct Therapy

The Facts About Heart Failure

How Heart Failure Patients Benefit from Dr. Rath's Vitamin Program

Dr. Rath's Vitamin Program Improves Heart Pumping Performance

The Facts About Heart Failure

Tens of millions of people worldwide are currently suffering from heart failure, resulting in shortness of breath, edema, and fatigue. The number of heart failure patients has tripled over the last four decades. The epidemic spread of this disease is largely due to the fact that until now the causes of heart failure have been insufficiently or not at all understood. In some cases heart failure is the result of a heart attack; in most cases, however, such as cardiomyopathies, heart failure develops without any prior cardiac event.

Conventional medicine is largely confined to treating the symptoms of heart failure. Diuretic drugs are given to flush out the water that is retained in the body because of the weak pumping function of the heart. The still insufficient understanding of the causes of heart failure also explains the unfavorable prognosis of this disease. Five years after a heart failure condition is diagnosed, only 50% of the patients are still alive. For many patients with heart failure, a heart transplant operation is the last resort. Most heart failure patients, however, die without ever having the option of such an operation.

Cellular Medicine provides a breakthrough in the understanding of the causes, the prevention, and the adjunct treatment of heart failure. The primary cause of heart failure is a deficiency of vitamins and other essential nutrients providing bioenergy to millions of heart muscle cells. These muscle cells are responsible for the contraction of the heart muscle and for optimum pumping of blood into the circulation. Deficiencies of vitamins and other essential nutrients impair the pumping performance of the heart, resulting in shortness of breath, edema, and fatigue

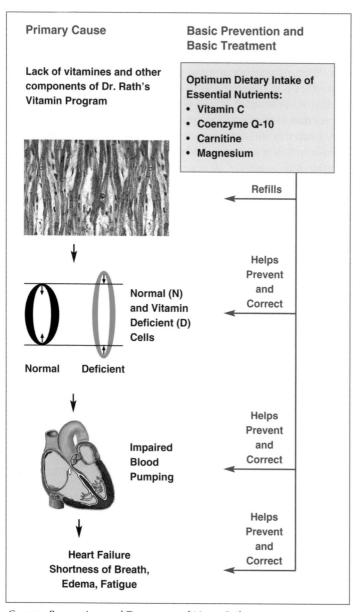

Primary Cause

Lack of vitamines and other components of Dr. Rath's Vitamin Program

Basic Prevention and Basic Treatment

Optimum Dietary Intake of Essential Nutrients:
- Vitamin C
- Coenzyme Q-10
- Carnitine
- Magnesium

Refills

Normal (N) and Vitamin Deficient (D) Cells

Normal   Deficient

Helps Prevent and Correct

Impaired Blood Pumping

Helps Prevent and Correct

Heart Failure Shortness of Breath, Edema, Fatigue

Helps Prevent and Correct

Causes, Prevention and Treatment of Heart Failure

Scientific research and clinical studies have already documented the particular value of carnitine, coenzyme Q-10, and other essential nutrients. These components of Dr. Rath's Vitamin Program improve the function of millions of heart muscle cells, the pumping function of the heart itself, and thereby, the quality of life of heart failure patients.

My recommendations for heart failure patients: start immediately with this vitamin program and inform your doctor about it. Follow this program in addition to your regular medication. Do not stop or alter your regular medication without consulting your doctor.

Prevention is better than treatment. The success of Dr. Rath's Vitamin Program in heart failure patients is based on the optimum supply of cell fuel for millions of heart muscle cells. A natural health program that is able to correct cardiovascular health conditions like heart failure in a natural way is, of course, your best choice to prevent these problems from developing in the first place.

How Heart Failure Patients Benefit from Dr. Rath's Vitamin Program

Following are grateful letters from heart failure patients following Dr. Rath's Vitamin Program. Please share this information with anyone you know who suffers from shortness of breath, edema or chronic fatigue. You may save a life.

Dear Dr. Rath:

I started following your vitamin program in January. **Since 1989 I have been suffering from congestive heart failure** *and to this day, I am still following the originally prescribed medication with good results. However, I noticed that I was unable to do any small effort or even walk a couple of blocks without suffering a chest pain and had to alleviate its intensity by ingesting a tablet. It was usual for me to take 3 to 5 tablets per 24 hours, the pain would surface sometimes with no apparent reason.*

After only four months on your vitamin program I not only rarely use the nitroglycerin tablets, but I am walking 1.1 mile every morning at a brisk pace, no shortness of breath, no chest pain.
Please keep in mind that my home town's altitude is 5280' above sea level. I'll be 75 next October. Thought you'd be interested to read about this.

Yours truly,
F.W.

Dear Dr. Rath

Our sister-in-law was diagnosed with **congestive heart failure** *and told by her physician to go home and get her affairs in order, sell her home and prepare to move into a nursing home because she was only going to get worse and wouldn't be able to care for herself.* **Her chest was full of fluids, she had to sleep sitting up, she was too weak to walk and her legs were swelling.**

She started your nutritional supplement program late in February, and **in three weeks she was feeling well enough to go out for dinner, get her hair done and put her house on the market.** *She has since moved into a nice retirement home and she goes everywhere the bus goes. She is so grateful, she has been given her life back and never wants to be without your vitamin program.*

Sincerely,
R.A

Dear Dr. Rath:

I am happy to report that your Dr. Rath's Vitamin Program has improved my life. **Now I can climb the stairs readily and without shortness of breath. I can also resume hiking for 3-4 miles a day without feeling tired and exhausted.** *I do have an energetic outlook towards life and sure it's due to your cardiovascular vitamin program.*

Thank you very much for all the research you have done and you are continuing to do for people with circulatory problems.

Sincerely,
A.G.

Dear Dr. Rath:

I am a 46 year old female. Six years ago I had a severe reaction to a prescription medication. The ultimate result of that is that I had severe congestive heart failure. I was diagnosed as having valvular regurgitation of the mitral, tricuspid and pulmonary valves (leaking of heart valves), as well as mitral valve prolapse. My clinical symptoms were extreme fatigue, shortness of breath, edema, tachycardia and pulmonary edema.

Since following your vitamin program I am now taking only a beta-blocker for medication. All others have been stopped. My symptoms are now occasional fatigue. **I do not have severe shortness of breath, I can carry on a conversation without sounding out of breath. I am able to exercise on a daily basis. There is no edema, tachycardia (rapid heartbeat), pulmonary congestion, etc.**

Your cardiovascular vitamin program has given me an entirely new look on the future, where at one time I did not feel that there would be a future

Sincerely, J.T.

Dear Dr. Rath:

For three months now I have been taking double the amounts of nutritional supplements recommended in your cardiovascular health program.

I just returned from my usual 4-mile walk at a brisk pace, up two small hills and around the neighborhood with no discomfort at all. **For the first time absolutely free of distress.** This feels like a miracle!

Best wishes, J.H.

Dear Dr. Rath:

I am a 36 year old female. **Since my late 20's I have experienced arrhythmia, shortness of breath periods. I also had begun to have edema in my ankles.** *My heart rate was usually between 88 and 98. My blood pressure averaged 140/86. Being a nurse, I knew to discontinue salt and caffeine. Upon doing so, the symptoms improved for a while. The past few years, however, I was beginning to require medication and was about to get further medical attention to my cardiac changes when I was introduced to your cardiovascular vitamin program last February.*

Now, four months later, I no longer require medication for the edema, nor do I have any arrhythmia, shortness of breath, or palpitations. *I have always continued my aerobic exercise, which I was beginning to have difficulty in sustaining. However, my stamina has improved tremendously over these past few months. My heart rate now averages 78 and my blood pressure was 112/60 last week.*

Thank you!

Sincerely and in Good Health,
V.G.

Dear Dr. Rath:

I started your vitamin program the same week I read your book titled "Why Animals Don't Get Heart Attacks, But People Do." Unlike many things in this world, your presentations are so basic and simple that everyone can understand the principles involved. My hope is that everyone in this country and the world will receive your message and have the same good results that I do.

I have eliminated my diuretic medications completely and cut my blood pressure medication in half since I started following your vitamin program. *I'm now reading 120 over 78 at age 69 and I feel great. My doctor was surprised and pleased and told me by all means to continue the preventative health care path that started with your program. This program is unique and your patent on the technology to reverse heart disease without surgery is, as you say, like patenting nature — and it works.*

Thank you so much for your work and for sharing your research with so many people. The world will be a happier place because of you.

Sincerely,
B.B.

113

Heart Transplant Operation Called Off

After visiting with a heart failure patient and his cardiologist I personally wrote the following report about the health improvement of this patient. From now on heart failure patients around the world can benefit from this vitamin program providing essential bioenergy to their heart muscle cells.

G.P. is an entrepreneur in his fifties. **Three years ago his life was changed by a sudden occurrence of heart failure,** *a weakness of the heart muscle leading to a decreased pumping function and to an enlargement of the heart chambers. The patient could no longer fully meet his professional obligations and had to give up all his sports activities.* **On some days he felt so weak that he couldn't climb stairs and he had to hold his drinking glass with both hands.** *Because of the continued weak pumping function of the heart and the unfavorable prognosis of this disease, his cardiologist recommended a heart transplant operation: "I recommend you get a new heart."*

At this point the patient started to follow the vitamin program I developed. His physical strength improved gradually. **Soon he could again fulfill his professional obligations on a regular basis and was able to enjoy daily bicycle rides. Two months after starting to follow my recommendations his cardiologist noted a decrease in size of the previously enlarged heart in the echocardiography examination, another sign of a recovering heart muscle.** *One month later the patient was able to take a business trip abroad and he could attend to his business affairs without any physical limitations.*

Dr. Rath's Vitamin Program Improves Heart Pumping Performance

In a clinical study, we documented that Dr. Rath's Vitamin Program improves heart performance in heart failure patients. In this clinical pilot study, six patients aged 40 to 66 were included. Initially the heart performance of these patients was measured by means of echocardiography (ultrasound examination of the heart). This test measured how much blood the heart pumps into the circulation with every heartbeat (ejection fraction). In addition, the physical performance of the patients was assessed with a treadmill ergometer. Then the patients followed this vitamin program in addition to their regular medication. After two months on this program, echocardiographic and ergometric control examinations were conducted. With this nutritional supplement program, the ejection fraction and the physical performance increased on average by 20%. Thus, Dr. Rath's Vitamin Program improved heart performance beyond any prescription drug tested thus far.

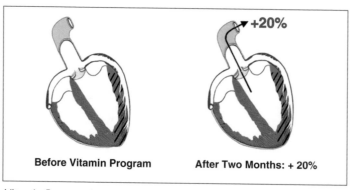

Before Vitamin Program   **After Two Months: + 20%**

Vitamin Program Improves Heart Pumping by 20%

The Fatal Consequences of Incomplete Treatment of Heart Failure

For decades, bias and skepticism have prevented medicine from correctly identifying the primary cause of heart failure. Today we know that a deficiency of vitamins and other essential nutrients in millions of heart muscle cells is the primary cause of heart failure. Moreover, the conventional treatment of heart failure patients is a good example of how an incomplete understanding of a disease can lead to a vicious cycle in which therapeutic measures can contribute to worsening the health problem.

A chronic deficiency of Dr. Rath's Vitamin Program in heart muscle cells causes decreased pumping function of the heart. This frequently leads to lower blood pressure and an impaired blood supply to different organs in the body, e.g., the kidneys. The primary role of the kidneys is to filter abandoned body water from the blood into the urine. With impaired blood flow through the kidneys, less water is filtered out and, instead of leaving the body via urine, it accumulates in the tissue of legs, lungs and other parts of the body (edema). In order to eliminate the abundant body water, doctors prescribe diuretic medication.

At this point, a vicious cycle is triggered in the conventional therapy of heart failure. Diuretics not only increase water elimination from the body, but also wash out water soluble vitamins, such as vitamin C and B vitamins, as well as important minerals and trace elements. Since vitamin deficiency is already the main cause of heart failure, diuretic medication further aggravates the underlying cause.

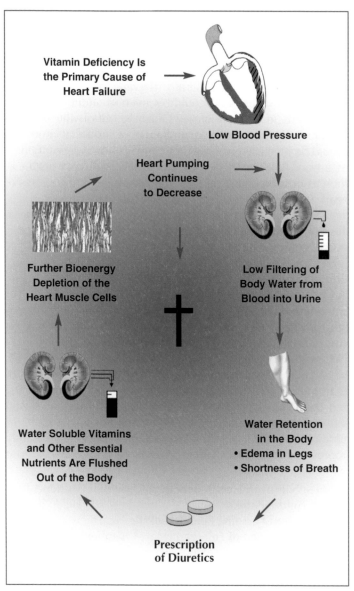

The Vicious Cycle Resulting from the Incomplete Treatment of Heart Failure

Now we understand why the prognosis of heart failure patients is so unfavorable. The future therapy of heart failure conditions is straightforward: the basic preventive and therapeutic measure is the supplementation of vitamins and other components of Dr. Rath's Vitamin Program. If water accumulates in a patient's body, diuretics should be given in addition. In order to compensate for the increased flushing out of water-soluble vitamins the daily supplementation of essential nutrients should be increased when diuretic medication is prescribed.

As a heart failure patient, you should talk with your doctor as soon as possible about the new understanding of the causes of heart failure and the new avenues of management documented in this book. A responsible physician will make use of this information and support you while you are following this essential nutrient program.

Clinical Studies: Vitamins and Heart Failure

In numerous clinical studies, compounds of Dr. Rath's Vitamin Program have been shown to greatly help people with shortness of breath, edema, and other heart failure conditions.

The most comprehensive clinical studies tested coenzyme Q-10 and carnitine, carrier molecules of bioenergy in millions of heart muscle cells. For example, Professors Langsjoen, Folkers, and their colleagues from the University of Texas in Austin showed that heart failure patients taking coenzyme Q-10 in addition to their regular medication could significantly improve their survival chances. After three years, 75% of those

Clinically Proven Health Benefits of Essential Nutrients for Heart Failure Patients
- **Improved Pumping Function of the Heart,**
- **Normalization of Enlarged Heart Chambers,**
- **Less Shortness of Breath,**
- **Less Edema,**
- **Improved Physical Performance,**
- **Significantly Longer Life Expectancy.**

patients who took coenzyme Q-10 in addition to their regular medication were still alive, whereas of those patients who took only their regular medication, 25% were still alive. In other words, every second patient in this study owed his or her life to coenzyme Q-10 supplementation.

Besides coenzyme Q-10 and carnitine, Dr. Rath's Vitamin Program also comprises other important natural substances which optimize the metabolism of heart muscle cells. This also explains the impressive success of our clinical pilot study in heart failure patients who started Dr. Rath's Vitamin Program. The following table summarizes the most important clinical studies with compounds of Dr. Rath's Vitamin Program.

Compounds of Dr. Rath's Vitamin Program	Reference
Coenzyme Q-10	Folkers, Langsjoen
Carnitine	Ghidini

Cellular Medicine Program for Patients with Heart Failure

In addition to the basic vitamin program (page 19), patients with shortness of breath, edema and chronic fatigue are recommended to take the following cellular bio-energy factors in higher dosages or in addition:

- **Vitamin C:** energy supply for the metabolism of each cell, supplies the bio-energy carrier molecules of the Vitamin B group with life-saving bio-energy.

- **Vitamin E:** anti-oxidative protection, protection of the cell membranes.

- **Vitamin B1, B2, B3, B5, B6, B12 and biotin:** bio-energy carriers of cellular metabolism, particularly for the heart muscle cells, improved heart function and heart pumping, improved physical endurance.

- **Coenzyme Q10:** most important element of the "respiration chain" of each cell, plays a particular role for improved heart muscle function because of the high bio-energy demand in the heart muscle cells.

- **Carnitine:** improved supply of bio-energy for the "power plants" (mitochondria) of millions of cells.

- **Taurine:** Taurine is a natural amino acid, its lack in the heart muscle cells is a particular frequent cause of heart failure.

Irregular Heartbeat (Arrhythmia)

6

Dr. Rath's Vitamin program for Prevention and Adjunct Therapy

Facts About Irregular Heartbeat

How Patients With Irregular Heartbeat Benefit from Dr. Rath's Vitamin Program

Clinical Studies in Arrhythmia Patients With Components of Dr. Rath's Vitamin Program

Facts About Irregular Heartbeat

Worldwide over 100 million people are suffering from irregular heartbeat. Irregular heartbeat is caused by a disturbance in the creation or conduction of the electrical impulse, responsible for a regular heartbeat. In some cases, these disturbances are caused by a damaged area of the heart muscle, e.g., after a heart attack. The textbooks of medicine, however, admit that in most cases the causes for irregular heart beat remain unknown. No wonder that irregular heartbeat conditions are spreading like an epidemic on a worldwide scale.

Conventional medicine has invented its own diagnostic terms to cover the fact that it does not know the origin of most arrhythmias. "Paroxysmal" arrhythmia means nothing else than "causes unknown." As a direct consequence, the therapeutic options of conventional medicine are confined to treating the symptoms of irregular heartbeat. Beta-blockers, calcium antagonists, and other anti-arrhythmic drugs are given to patients in the hope that they decrease the incidents of irregular heartbeat.

Slow forms of arrhythmias with long pauses between heartbeats are dealt with by implanting a pacemaker. In other cases, heart muscle tissue that creates or conducts uncoordinated electrical impulses is cauterized (burned) and thereby eliminated as a focus of the electrical disturbance in the heart muscle. Lacking an understanding of the primary cause of irregular heartbeat, the therapeutic approaches by conventional medicine are not specific and therefore frequently fail.

Modern Cellular Medicine now provides a decisive breakthrough in our understanding of the causes, prevention, and adjunct therapy of irregular heartbeat. The most frequent cause of irregular heartbeat is a chronic deficiency in vitamins and other essential nutrients in millions of electrical heart muscle cells. Long term, these deficiencies of essential nutrients directly cause, or aggravate, disturbances in the creation or conduction of the electrical impulses triggering the heartbeat.

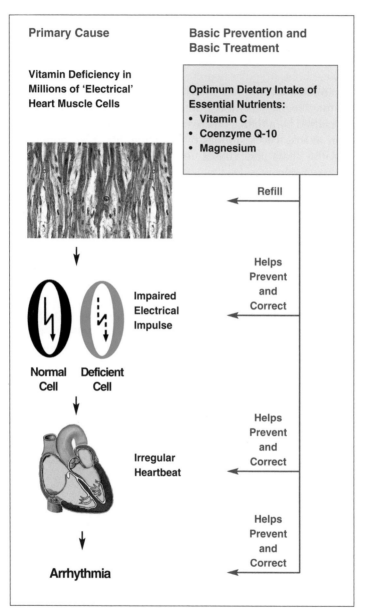

Primary Cause	Basic Prevention and Basic Treatment
Vitamin Deficiency in Millions of 'Electrical' Heart Muscle Cells	**Optimum Dietary Intake of Essential Nutrients:** • Vitamin C • Coenzyme Q-10 • Magnesium

Refill

Impaired Electrical Impulse

Helps Prevent and Correct

Normal Cell   Deficient Cell

Irregular Heartbeat

Helps Prevent and Correct

Arrhythmia

Helps Prevent and Correct

Causes, Prevention and Treatment of Irregular Heartbeat

Thus, the primary method for preventing and correcting irregular heart beat conditions is an optimum supply of vitamins and other components of Dr. Rath's Vitamin Program.

Scientific research and clinical studies have already documented the value of magnesium, carnitine, coenzyme Q-10, and other important components of Dr. Rath's Vitamin Program in helping to normalize different forms of irregular heart beat and thereby improving the quality of life for patients.

My recommendations for patients with irregular heartbeat: start as soon as possible with this vitamin program and inform your doctor about it. Take these essential nutrients in addition to your regular medication. Do not stop or alter your regular medication on your own. Any changes of anti-arrhythmic medication can have serious consequences for your heartbeat and should be done only in consultation with your doctor.

Prevention is better than treatment. A natural cardiovascular program which helps to correct severe health conditions such as irregular heart beat is, of course, also your best choice for preventing irregular heart beat in the first place.

124

How Patients With Irregular Heartbeat Benefit from Dr. Rath's Vitamin Program

Please share the following letters and this book with anyone you know suffering from irregular heartbeat. By doing so you may be able to greatly improve the quality of life of a person or even save a life.

Dear Dr. Rath:

Two months ago I was experiencing loud heartbeats, tachycardia and irregular beating of the heart. *I saw my doctor who promptly put me on an anti-arrhythmic drug. I can honestly say the medication did me absolutely no good.*

Then, I started to follow your vitamin program. What a smart decision that was! **Within a few days, the tachycardia stopped and I've not experienced any loud or irregular heartbeats.** *It's like a miracle. It must be the combination of nutrients in your program because I had been taking Coenzyme Q10 separately from my regular vitamins. I tell everyone I know about the benefits of your program. Because of your research, I'm able to continue working.*

Sincerely, B.M.

Dear Dr. Rath:

In February I introduced my 74 year old grandmother to your cardiovascular vitamin program. **Her slow and irregular heart beat had led her doctor to begin preliminary preparations to install a pacemaker.**

After about three weeks on your program her heart action was sufficiently improved to cause the doctor to postpone this procedure. *This lady is now a faithful follower of your cardiovascular health program and, although she faces other medical challenges, her heart condition continues to improve, and the use of a pacemaker is no longer being considered.*

Sincerely, K.C

Dear. Dr. Rath:

*I am excited to tell you of my experience. I am a 60 year old female who has fought hypertension for the past 20 years with many different types of medications which would work for a while, then become ineffective and start giving me problems. In November of 1993 new symptoms began for which I was referred to a cardiologist who determined I was well on my way to a pacemaker. He decided not to treat this aggressively, but instead, through medication. I have avoided surgery. **In February of this year I began experiencing prolonged bouts of tachycardia, and was prescribed new, additional medication.***

*In March I was introduced to your cardiovascular vitamin program. Although I was skeptical, I decided to give it a try. I've just started my third month on your program and have been able to reduce my blood pressure medication by one-third. **The episodes of tachycardia have decreased dramatically, both in intensity and duration. If an episode occurs, it is almost insignificant. At the same time, I have also noted a dramatic effect in that my ankles are no longer swelling at the end of a workday.***

Following my last lab work, my doctor told me "Your numbers look like someone one-half your age." Needless to say I am a staunch believer in your vitamin program.

Sincerely,
F.S.

Dear Dr. Rath:

I am 54 years of age and have had a very irregular heartbeat for at least 20 years. This was diagnosed as second degree electrical heart block. I have never taken any medication for this. I have had a stress test done approximately every 2 years and the heart block showed up on the EKG. I was told that as long as my heartbeat becomes regular when I exercised that I did not need any other treatment.

In June I even went back to the doctor where I had my last EKG done so there would be a basis for comparison. **The doctor found that there was no longer any arrhythmia seen. I have enclosed a copy of his report.** I am sure that your cardiovascular vitamin program is responsible for the correction of my irregular heartbeat, as I had not changed my lifestyle in any other respect

Sincerely,
T.H

Dear Dr. Rath:

How delightful, after following your cardiovascular health program for just 2 months, one notices the absence of irregular heartbeats, and the freedom to breathe freely. Confidence is restored as one has increased vigor and endurance. In a word, one spends less time thinking about the heart and more time enjoying life.

Your cardiovascular health program has become the answer for resolving coronary problems. I am happy to have this opportunity of expressing my gratitude for your advanced medical research and for your cardiovascular health program.

Yours sincerely,
J.S.

Dear Dr. Rath:

Thank you for developing your essential nutrient program, which I am currently following. **Several years ago I was diagnosed as having Hyperkinetic Heart Syndrome.** *I took medication for a few years, but did not like how I felt — too slowed down and not able to respond quickly to physical exertion.*

During times of great stress, I would have pounding, irregular, racing heartbeats at nighttime when I am trying to fall asleep. *Also, when confronted with a stressful encounter during the day, my heart would immediately jump into a racing, pounding episode. I heard your lecture in May. I immediately read two of your books.*

A week later I began following your cardiovascular vitamin program and within a few days, I was no longer experiencing pounding, irregular, racing heartbeats at bedtime. Within a week I noticed that when confronted with a stressful encounter during the day, my heart did not jump into racing and pounding episode.

I have taken vitamin, mineral, herbal supplements for several years, but have never had this amazing result before now! Thank you so very much!

Yours truly,
C.M.

Dear Dr. Rath:

I am a thirty-five year old medical professional. One and one half years ago, due to severe distress to my professional and personal life, **I suddenly experienced bouts of supraventricular tachycardia (fast heartbeat) which forced me into the emergency room every two months** *over a six month period. My average heart rate would be 230 beats per minute. This condition was life threatening and after my third episode I was referred to the chief of cardiology at the largest hospital in town. After a thorough evaluation, it was concluded that I was not suffering from 'anxiety' but a primary electrical problem with my heart and supraventricular tachycardia could occur anytime.*

Therefore, he recommended a surgical procedure called Cardiac Ablation. This procedure involved the insertion of catheters into my subclavian and femoral arteries and threading them to the sinus and atrioventricular nodal regions of the heart and with a DC current, cauterize certain regions of the heart theorized to cause this aberrant electrical circuit. Although this procedure was definitely indicated, I was too weakened from my recent bout with tachycardia to consider immediate surgery. I therefore resolved to improve my health by strengthening myself nutritionally with vitamins, minerals, herbal and homeopathic formulas.

My research lead me to your cardiovascular health program. Your formulation was specific to my health needs and it saved me much time considering I would have purchased many bottles of isolated ingredients that are all found in your program. Therefore, I embarked on a religious program of supplementation of the essential nutrients you recommend. **It has been one and one half years from my last episode. I have increased energy, little to no chest pain. I look and feel much better.** *I attribute my success and health to your program.*

Sincerely,
S.S.

Clinical Studies in Arrhythmia Patients With Components of Dr. Rath's Vitamin Program

In addition to these patient reports clinical studies have documented the health benefits of various components of Dr. Rath's Vitamin Program in patients with irregular heart beat. The following table summarizes some of the most important clinical studies in this area:

Components of Dr. Rath's Vitamin Program	References
Magnesium	England, Turlapaty
Carnitine	Rizzon

For an adjunct Cellular Medicine program for patients with irregular heart beat see page 116. Bio-energy factors that help millions of heart muscle cells to pump, also optimize the function of "electrical" heart cells.

Diabetes

7

Dr. Rath's Vitamin program for Prevention and Adjunct Therapy

The Facts About Adult Diabetes

How Diabetic Patients Benefit from Dr. Rath's Vitamin Program

Background Information on Dr. Rath's Vitamin Program for Diabetes

The Facts About Adult Diabetes

Worldwide over one hundred million people are suffering from diabetes. Diabetic disorders have a genetic background and are divided into two types: juvenile and adult diabetes. Juvenile diabetes is generally caused by an inborn defect that leads to an insufficient production of insulin in the body and requires regular insulin injections to control blood sugar levels. The majority of diabetic patients, however, develop this disease as adults. Adult forms of diabetes also have a genetic background. The causes, however, which trigger the outbreak of the disease in these patients at any stage of their adult lives, have been unknown. It is, therefore, not surprising that diabetes is yet another disease that is still expanding on a worldwide scale.

Conventional medicine is confined to treating the symptoms of adult diabetes by lowering elevated blood levels of sugar. However, cardiovascular diseases and other diabetic complications occur even in those patients with controlled blood sugar levels. Thus, lowering of blood sugar levels is a necessary, but insufficient and incomplete treatment of diabetic disorders.

Modern Cellular Medicine now provides a breakthrough in our understanding of the causes, the prevention, and the adjunct therapy of adult diabetes. Adult onset diabetes is frequently caused or aggravated by a deficiency of certain vitamins and other essential nutrients in millions of cells in the pancreas (the organ that produces insulin), the liver, and the blood vessel walls, as well as other organs. On the basis of an inherited diabetic disorder, deficiencies of vitamins and other essential nutrients can trigger a diabetic metabolism and the onset of adult diabetes. Vice versa, optimum intake of vitamins and other ingredients in Dr. Rath's Vitamin Program can prevent the onset of adult diabetes and correct, at least in part, existing diabetes and its complications.

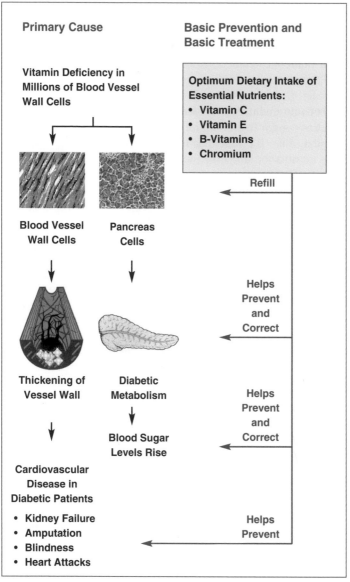

Primary Cause

Basic Prevention and Basic Treatment

Vitamin Deficiency in Millions of Blood Vessel Wall Cells

Optimum Dietary Intake of Essential Nutrients:
- **Vitamin C**
- **Vitamin E**
- **B-Vitamins**
- **Chromium**

Blood Vessel Wall Cells   **Pancreas Cells**

Refill

Thickening of Vessel Wall   **Diabetic Metabolism**

Helps Prevent and Correct

Blood Sugar Levels Rise

Helps Prevent and Correct

Cardiovascular Disease in Diabetic Patients
- **Kidney Failure**
- **Amputation**
- **Blindness**
- **Heart Attacks**

Helps Prevent

Causes, Prevention and Treatment of Cardiovascular Complications in Diabetes

133

Scientific research and clinical studies have documented the particular value of vitamin C, vitamin E, certain B vitamins, chromium, and other essential nutrients in helping to normalize a diabetic metabolism and to prevent cardiovascular disease.

My recommendations for diabetic patients: Start immediately with this program of essential nutrients and inform your doctor about it. Take the essential nutrients in addition to your diabetes medication and take them regularly. High amounts of vitamin C, for example, can spare insulin units and you should have additional blood sugar controls at the beginning of this vitamin program. Do not stop or change any prescription medication without consulting your doctor.

Prevention is better than treatment. The success of Dr. Rath's Vitamin Program in diabetic patients is based on the fact that it eliminates a deficiency of cell fuel in the pancreas, liver, and blood vessel wall cells. A natural cardiovascular health program that is able to correct severe conditions such as diabetes is, of course, your best choice to prevent diabetes and its cardiovascular complications in the first place.

How Diabetic Patients Benefit from Dr. Rath's Vitamin Program

The following sequence documents a selection of letters from patients with diabetic disorders. I encourage you to share these letters and the contents of this book with anyone you know suffering from diabetes. By doing so, you can help prevent heart attacks, strokes, blindness, and other organ failure in these patients.

Dear Dr. Rath,

*I started following your cardiovascular vitamin program three months ago. **I'm 29 years old and was recently diagnosed with Type II Diabetes. Since following your program on a regular basis, I have found my blood glucose level to remain around 100, even when under stress, which previously raised my blood glucose level.***

Your vitamin program and 1-2 extra grams of vitamin C have relieved the primary negative symptoms that I have experienced such as weakness from low blood sugar levels, pain in the right side from high blood sugar, and painful urination from the higher blood sugar levels.

I have found only positive results from your program.

Sincerely,
A.M.

Dear Dr. Rath,

I would like to share my story with you in hope that the informa-tion will help other diabetics with similar conditions. *More importantly, I am hopeful this information will keep other diabet-ics from ever having to experience the frustration and debilitating pain involved with peripheral neuropathy, as I have.*

For many years I have been suffering from diabetes and diabetic neuropathy. My toes were turning dark blue and purple, and I did not have any feeling in them. The prognosis was very grim; if my condition did not get better I could lose my toes, if not my feet.

I was looking for a treatment that would help this condition. Then I learned about your cardiovascular vitamin program. After about a week of following your program, to my delight, my toes became a bright maroon color instead of blue and purple, and much to my amazement hair was beginning to grow again on my legs telling me that blood was reaching the hair follicles.

By the 2nd week my legs were not cramping as often or as badly but by the end of the 3rd week my feet and ankles were giving me excruciating pain. I mentioned what was happening to me to a friend who is a druggist. **He happily told me that he believed the nerves were regenerating. The feeling, which has been absent for several years, is coming back in my feet. I can feel the inside of my shoes again. I am now starting the 3rd month on your program.**

Your nutritional supplement program coupled with my sta-tionery bicycle and insulin adjustments, suggestions from my dietitian, are all elements in helping me fight the battle and win-ning.

Very sincerely yours,
M.J.

Dear Dr. Rath,

I am a 55 year old male Caucasian, weighing 154 pounds. I lead a very sedentary lifestyle spending most of my time sitting behind a desk in front of a computer. **About 20 years ago I was diagnosed a type II (adult onset) Diabetic and placed on oral medication and dietary restrictions to control my blood sugar level.** *These precautions seemed to work up to about a year ago when my blood sugar went to about 260 where it remains fairly steady, a fact that caused my physician (an endocrinologist) to change my medication and to drastically increase my dosage. He is currently seeing me on a monthly basis in an attempt to stabilize my condition.*

In February of 1986, I underwent quintuple bypass surgery to remedy severe angina and all the other symptoms of cardiovascular disease. Since the operation I have not experienced any symptoms such as pain, shortness of breath or irregular heartbeat.
I have followed your cardiovascular vitamin program every day as prescribed in your instructions for exactly 2 months, and since approximately 2 weeks ago I noticed a dramatic increase in my energy level. I can accomplish much more in my daily work, I find myself eager to stay up late, and recently I found myself out dancing late at night with my wife, just as I used to do about 20 years ago. *Since nothing in my daily routine has changed except the advent of your program. I must conclude that this newly found "fountain of youth" is a direct result of your program.*

In closing, I am grateful to your vitamin program for the improvements shown thus far. Please feel free to use this letter, or any part thereof as a testimonial in your efforts.

Sincerely,
N.M.

137

Dear Dr. Rath:

I am a 69-year-old woman, employed full-time in a position that requires close attention to detail and considerable adjustment to time constraints.

*At the beginning of last year, during my annual physical examination, my physician stated that **I had developed glucose intolerance and that the ultimate result would be diabetes unless I immediately began countermeasures.***

I then met with a diabetic counselor, and gave her all the information that I possessed concerning your cardiovascular vitamin program. Following this consultation, I started your program. I also modified my diet, began to exercise regularly, and have lost a substantial amount of weight.

Now, one year later, my doctor informs me that my diabetic condition is in full remission. Furthermore, my blood pressure is in the normal range, my blood tests are all excellent, my energy has noticeably increased, and my general condition is once again first rate.

Dr. Rath, I attribute the turnaround in my health to your vitamin program.

Thank you.
M.B.

Further Health Information Related to Dr. Rath's Vitamin Program in Diabetes

Diabetes is a particularly malicious metabolic disorder. Circulatory problems and clogging can occur in virtually every part of the 60,000-mile-long vessel pipeline.

Frequent Cardiovascular Complications in Diabetic Patients:
- Blindness from clogging of the arteries of the eyes
- Kidney failure from kidney artery clogging, requiring dialysis
- Gangrene from clogging of the small arteries of the toes
- Heart attacks from clogging of the coronary arteries
- Strokes from clogging of brain arteries

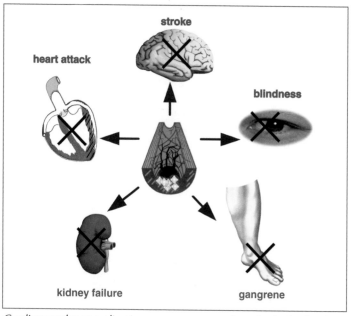

Cardiovascular complications can occur anywhere in the body of a diabetic

How Diabetic Cardiovascular Disease Develops

The key to understanding cardiovascular disease in diabetics is the similarity in the molecular structure of vitamin C and sugar (glucose) molecules. This similarity leads to a metabolic confusion, with severe consequences:

Column A on the next page shows that the cells of our blood vessel walls contain tiny biological pumps specialized for pumping sugar *and* vitamin C molecules from the blood stream into the blood vessel wall. In a healthy person, these pumps transport an optimum amount of sugar and vitamin C molecules into the blood vessel wall, enabling normal function of the wall and preventing cardiovascular disease.

Column B shows the situation in a diabetic patient. Because of the high sugar concentration in the blood, the sugar+vitamin C pumps are overloaded with sugar molecules. This leads to an overload of sugar and, at the same time, to a deficiency of vitamin C inside the blood vessel walls. The consequence of these mechanisms is a thickening of the walls throughout the blood vessel pipeline, putting any organ at risk for infarctions.

Column C shows the decisive measure for preventing cardiovascular complications in diabetes. An optimum daily intake of Dr. Rath's Vitamin Program and one or more additional grams of vitamin C help to normalize the imbalance between vitamin and sugar metabolism. Optimum vitamin supply will soon become the basic preventive and therapeutic measure for diabetes.

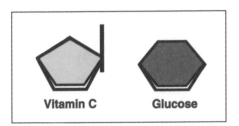

Vitamin C and sugar (glucose) molecules look confusingly similar

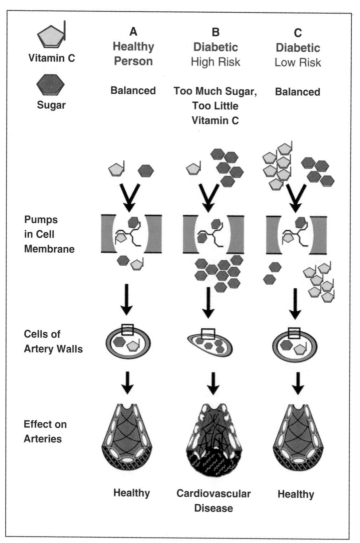

Vitamin C Is the Basic Therapy for Diabetic Patients to Prevent Cardiovascular Disease

Vitamin C Lowers Blood Sugar Levels and Insulin Requirement

Clinical studies show that in diabetic patients vitamin C contributes not only to prevention of cardiovascular complications, but also helps to normalize the imbalance in the glucose metabolism. Professor Pfleger and his colleagues from the University of Vienna published the results of a remarkable clinical study. They showed that diabetic patients taking 300 to 500 mg of vitamin C a day could significantly improve glucose balance. Blood sugar levels could be lowered on average by 30%, daily insulin requirements by 27%, and sugar excretion in the urine could be almost eliminated.

It is amazing that this study was published in 1937 in a leading European journal for internal medicine. If the results of this important study had been followed up and documented in medical textbooks, millions of lives would have been saved and cardiovascular disease would no longer threaten diabetic patients.

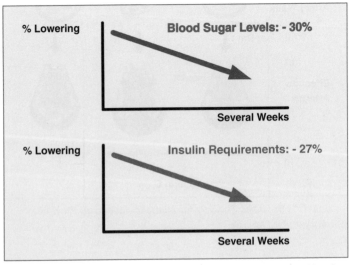

Clinical Study in Diabetic Patients Shows: Vitamin C Lowers Blood Sugar Levels and Insulin Requirement

Study Shows: the More Vitamin C, the Less Insulin

Diabetic patients can significantly lower their daily insulin requirements by increasing their daily intake of vitamin C. This is the result of a clinical case study conducted at the renowned Stanford University in California. Dr. Dice, the lead author of the study, was the diabetic patient of this case report. At the beginning of the study Dr. Dice injected 32 units of insulin per day. During the three-week study, he gradually increased the daily intake of vitamin C until he reached 11 grams per day on the 23rd day. The vitamin C was divided in small amounts and taken throughout the day to increase its absorption in the body. By the 23rd day, his insulin requirement had dropped from 32 units to 5 units per day. Thus, for every additional gram of dietary vitamin C supplementation, Dr. Dice could spare 2.5 insulin units.

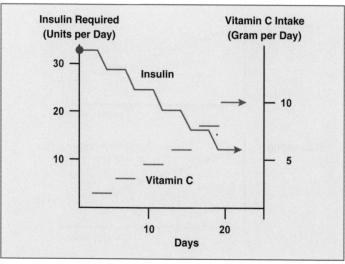

Clinical Study Shows: Each Additional Gram of Vitamin C Can Spare 2.5 Units of Insulin

Clinical Studies

Different components of Dr. Rath's Vitamin Program have been shown in clinical studies to have health benefits for diabetic patients:

Component of Dr. Rath's Vitamin Program	References
Vitamin C	Mann, Som, Stankova, Stepp
Vitamin E	Paolisso
Magnesium	McNair, Mather
Chromium	Liu, Riales

Cellular Medicine Program for Patients with Diabetes

In addition to the basic vitamin program (page 18-19) patients with diabetes and diabetic complications are recommended to take the following cellular bio-energy factors in higher dosages or separately:

- Vitamin C: corrects the cellular imbalance caused by elevated blood sugar levels, contributes to lower insulin requirements, decreases glucose elimination in the urine and, above all, protects the artery walls.

- Vitamin E: anti-oxidant protection, protection of the cell membranes.

- Vitamin B1, B2, B3, B5, B6, B12 and Biotin: bio-energy carriers of cellular metabolism, improved metabolic efficacy, particularly of the liver cells, the central unit of the body metabolism.

- Chromium: trace element, functioning as a bio-catalyst for optimum metabolism of glucose and insulin.

- Inositol: component of lecithin, an important component of each cell membrane, essential for optimum metabolic transport and supply of each cell with nutrients and other bio molecules.

- Choline: component of lecithin, important for the metabolic transport and cellular supply of millions of cells.

Please note: the most important aim is to provide optimum protection for your artery walls, not to completely substitute for your insulin. In many cases, particularly in patients with *inherited* (juvenile) insulin deficiency, this will not be possible.

Notes

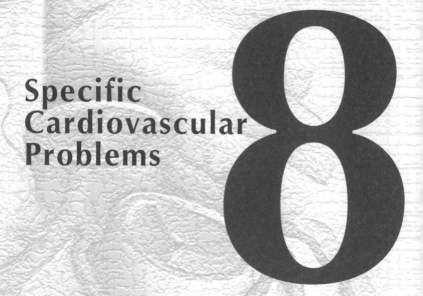

Specific Cardiovascular Problems

8

Dr. Rath's Vitamin program for Prevention and Adjunct Therapy

How Dr. Rath's Vitamin Program Can Help Ameliorate Angina Pectoris

Dr. Rath's Vitamin Program After a Heart Attack

Dr. Rath's Vitamin Program and Coronary Bypass Surgery

Dr. Rath's Vitamin Program and Coronary Angioplasty

How Dr. Rath's Vitamin Program Can Help Ameliorate Angina Pectoris

Angina pectoris is the typical alarm signal for atherosclerotic deposits in the coronary arteries and decreased blood supply to millions of heart muscle cells. Angina pectoris is typically a sharp pain in the middle of the chest which frequently radiates into the left arm. Because there are many atypical forms of angina pectoris, I advise you to consult with a physician about any form of unclear chest pain.

Dr. Rath's Vitamin Program can help to improve the blood supply to the heart muscle cells by providing oxygen and nutrients, thereby decreasing angina pectoris. Several essential nutrients in this program work together to achieve this aim. The most important ingredients are the following:

- Optimum supply of vitamin C and magnesium, as well as the natural amino acid, arginine, to aid widening of the coronary arteries and thereby to an increased blood supply through the coronary arteries to the heart muscle cells.

- Carnitine, coenzyme Q10, B vitamins, certain minerals, and trace elements improve the performance of the heart muscle cells, the pumping function of the heart, the pressure by which the blood is pumped through the coronary arteries and, thereby, the supply of oxygen and nutrients to the heart muscle cells.

- Over a period of many months, vitamin C, lysine and proline initiate the healing process of the artery walls and the decrease of atherosclerotic deposits by the mechanisms described in detail earlier in this book.

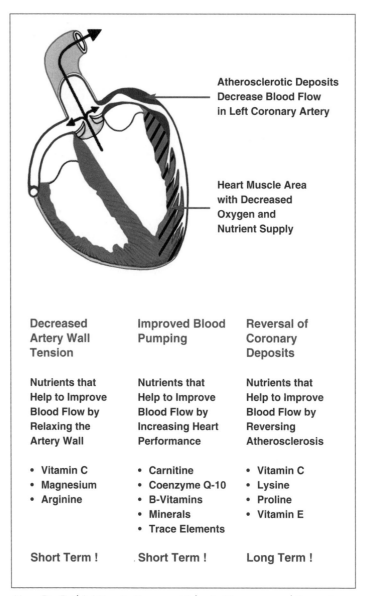

Atherosclerotic Deposits Decrease Blood Flow in Left Coronary Artery

Heart Muscle Area with Decreased Oxygen and Nutrient Supply

Decreased Artery Wall Tension	**Improved Blood Pumping**	**Reversal of Coronary Deposits**
Nutrients that Help to Improve Blood Flow by Relaxing the Artery Wall	Nutrients that Help to Improve Blood Flow by Increasing Heart Performance	Nutrients that Help to Improve Blood Flow by Reversing Atherosclerosis
• Vitamin C • Magnesium • Arginine	• Carnitine • Coenzyme Q-10 • B-Vitamins • Minerals • Trace Elements	• Vitamin C • Lysine • Proline • Vitamin E
Short Term !	**Short Term !**	**Long Term !**

How Dr. Rath's Vitamin Program Helps to Decrease and Prevent Angina Pectoris

How Patients with Angina Pectoris Benefit from Dr. Rath's Vitamin Program

The following section presents a selection of letters from patients with coronary artery disease and angina pectoris. This book documents the success with Dr. Rath's Vitamin Program enabling angina pectoris patients around the world to take advantage of this medical breakthrough and to improve their quality of life.

Dear Dr. Rath,

I am so happy to tell you of the use of your cardiovascular health program and how I feel that it has saved my life. Last September I had gone to the university to watch a football game and could not make it up the steps in the stadium despite wearing a nitroglycerin patch, and **by October last year I could not walk 100 yards without the pain of angina.**

I found out about your discovery and took it triple strength four times a day for three weeks and by Thanksgiving I had forgotten I had a heart problem. Now, in July of this year I am working without pain and feeling super!

Too bad you did not have the patent before I had undergone two bypass surgeries.

Thanks for more life,
J.G.

Dear Dr. Rath:

In May 1992 some extraordinary physical exertion on my part brought on pain that was especially noticeable in my left arm and left shoulder. **By the next morning the pain had progressed to the middle of my chest and I then recognized the pain as angina.** *Immediately, I started a series of treatments. During the treatments and after, I started a walking program. Although my walking did not cause any severe angina pain, there was still tightness in my chest and a necessity to slow down my pace because of a shortness of breath.*

It wasn't until I started following your cardiovascular health recommendations that I experienced a difference. Remarkably, within a month the discomfort from walking had entirely disappeared. Presently, I am walking 2.5 miles at least 3 days per week at a fast clip with no discomfort whatsoever.

I am cognizant that the buildup within my blood vessel walls occurred over a long time period, so I am prepared to continue following your recommendations on a continuous basis. It's a small price to pay for arteries that are free of atherosclerotic deposits.

Thanks for your cardiovascular recommendations! I feel that you have made a tremendous scientific breakthrough in the treatment of heart disease.

Sincerely,
M.L.

Dear Dr. Rath:

I started following your cardiovascular health program last August after I was diagnosed as having severe heart disease. **I had angina for 8 years. Now, nearly a year later, I feel fine and have very slight angina infrequently, plus I walk 3.6 miles daily and don't have any restrictions.**

Sincerely, M.B

Dear Dr. Rath,

Since following your vitamin program on a regular basis, I notice a significant increase in my physical and mental health. I have no present indications of angina, and my ability to walk vigorously around the hills that are in my neighborhood is most encouraging. No huffing and puffing and pausing to catch my breath, as before.

I am able to walk around my neighborhood hills without interrupting the rhythm and flow of my conversation. I also pursue a very modest weight loss program, eating much less than before — with no loss of energy.

I feel that your program is most significant in all this.

Sincerely yours   R.A.

Dear Dr. Rath:

I had been having chest pain (angina pectoris) for several years on the average of about every three weeks. **Since I started your vitamin program over 90 days ago, I have only had chest pain one time, which was about three weeks after starting your program.**

I feel that proper nutrition can prevent eighty percent of our health problems.

Sincerely, B.T.

Clinical Studies With Components of Dr. Rath's Vitamin Program in Angina Pectoris Patients

Additional reports from patients with angina pectoris about health improvements with Dr. Rath's Vitamin Program are documented in Section 2.1 of this book. In addition, an increasing number of clinical studies with various components of Dr. Rath's Vitamin Program confirm that a decrease of angina pectoris is possible by supplementation with these essential nutrients. These clinically tested nutritional supplements are included in Dr. Rath's Vitamin Program.

The following table summarizes some of the most important of these clinical studies:

Components of Dr. Rath's Vitamin Program	References
Vitamin C, Vitamin E	Riemersma
Beta carotene	Riemersma
Carnitine	Ferrari, Opie
Coenzyme Q10	Folkers, Kamikawa
Magnesium	Iseri, Teo

Dr. Rath's Vitamin Program After a Heart Attack

What Are the Consequences of a Heart Attack?

In the previous sections, we have seen how atherosclerotic deposits in coronary arteries reduce the blood flow, thereby causing the heart muscle to suffocate. A heart attack is caused by the complete clogging of a coronary artery and by the total cut-off of heart muscle cells from oxygen and nutrient supply. Unless medical assistance is available quickly, millions of heart muscle cells which are cut off from the blood supply die. The larger the size of the dead heart muscle area, the greater the complications. Two main complications generally result from a heart attack:

- **Impaired pumping function (heart failure):** The sector of the heart muscle that died impairs the pumping function of the heart. The consequences are an impaired circulation, shortness of breath, edema, and decreased physical capacity. For example, the effect of the failure of 25% of the heart muscles after a heart attack is like a four-cylinder motor running on three cylinders.

- **Impaired electrical conduction (irregular heartbeat):** In a similar way, the electrical cells of the heart can be affected by a heart attack. This can lead to various forms of irregular heart beat. Severe forms of arrhythmia are the most frequent causes of death during and after a heart attack.

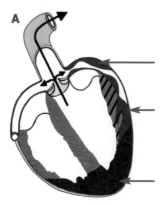

**Atherosclerotic Plaques
in the Coronary Arteries are the
Underlying Cause**

**Complete Clogging of the
Artery Triggers Heart Attack**

**Death of Heart Muscle
Tissue Can Cause**
- **Decreased Pumping**
- **Irregular Heartbeat**

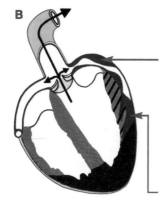

**Halt of Atherosclerosis Helps
Prevent Further Heart Attacks**
- **Vitamin C**
- **Lysine/Proline**
- **Antioxidants**

**Optimizing Function of Heart
Muscle Tissue that Is Still Alive**
- **Carnitine**
- **Coenzyme Q-10**
- **B-Vitamins**
- **Minerals and Trace Elements**

A: The Consequences of a Heart Attack

B: How Dr. Rath's Vitamin Program Contributes to an Improved
Quality of Life after a Heart Attack

155

How Dr. Rath's Vitamin Program Can Improve Quality of Life After a Heart Attack

Anybody suffering a heart attack should be immediately transported to the nearest hospital. The sooner a patient receives proper medical attention, the greater the chance of limiting the lasting damage to the heart muscle cells. If a heart attack occurred some time ago, you should continue to consult regularly with your physician. In addition, Dr. Rath's Vitamin Program can help in the following way to improve the quality of life:

- **Halting the development of atherosclerotic deposits** in the coronary arteries, thereby helping to prevent further heart attacks. The most important components of Dr. Rath's Vitamin Program contributing to this effect are vitamin C and other antioxidant vitamins, as well as the amino acids lysine and proline.

- **Optimizing the function of heart muscle cells still alive.** This is particularly important in the heart muscle area immediately bordering the dead heart muscle area, where millions of cells are still functioning, but at an impaired level. The most important components of Dr. Rath's Vitamin Program contributing to this effect are the B vitamins, carnitine, coenzyme Q10, as well as many minerals and trace elements.

Thus, it is not surprising that heart attack patients who start on Dr. Rath's Vitamin Program experience significant health improvements.

How Patients Who Have Suffered a Heart Attack Can Benefit from Dr. Rath's Vitamin Program

Following are sample letters from patients who benefitted from starting Dr. Rath's Vitamin Program after suffering a heart attack. Additional letters are documented throughout this book. Please share this important information with anyone you know who has suffered a heart attack. You may help prevent further heart attacks.

Dear Dr. Rath:

In January of this year I began experiencing chest pains when exercising. In April my doctor told me, on the basis of an EKG, that I had suffered a heart attack. He continued prescribing a beta-blocker, which I had been taking for high blood pressure for many years.

In May I started following your cardiovascular vitamin program and also went on a very strict vegetarian, no-fat diet. My chest pain during exercise began to lessen after just two weeks of this regimen. I have now been on a diet and your vitamin program for 2 months, and I now have no chest pain or breathlessness at all, even when cycling or walking energetically for several hours at a time. I also feel better than I have felt for years, with lots of energy and high spirits.

My confidence level in my heart condition is so good that I no longer carry nitroglycerin pills with me when setting out on a bicycle ride or a walk. I feel young and bright. Since the only change in my lifestyle has been your cardiovascular health program and diet, I have to say that one or both of these factors have caused this dramatic change in my health. For what it is worth, I tend to think that the combination of both these factors together is what has caused my health to improve.

Yours truly,
K.P.

Dear Dr. Rath:

My dad was diagnosed with blockages of the heart in October last year. He also suffered from angina and from arrhythmia. *He could not walk a block without concern for his ability to make it home again. My dad was concerned for his life; because he had two ischemic events (four years ago) along with being diabetic and being eighty years of age, his medical advisors ruled out an invasive procedure as a remedy.*

When I was first made aware of your breakthrough noninvasive therapy, I could not believe our good fortune. Immediately we placed dad on your cardiovascular vitamin program. Within a day he reported good results. " I feel good!" was his response after the first day. The second day he told me that his energy level had increased significantly. "I was able to work in the garage all day today without getting tired. **The third day and dad had walked a block and returned without difficulty – no pains, fatigue or apprehension.**

The chest pains went away by December and in January on our way to the cardiologist's office, dad, having forgotten his essential nutrients for his doctors' inspection and review, ran back into the house to retrieve them. I got so excited by the event that I had immediately started calling people on my car phone to share with them what I had just witnessed – a miracle!

My dad's heart no longer skips a beat, his angina is gone, *his blood flows freely when he proudly donates blood samples. His doctors are amazed with his new- found state of health. And we are very, very happy. Last week my dad took a ten-block walk without difficulty; he is proud and grateful.*

Thank you, Dr. Rath. Your research has given my dad back his life.

Sincerely, M.T.

Dr. Rath's Vitamin Program and Coronary Bypass Surgery

What Is a Coronary Bypass Operation?

A coronary bypass operation becomes necessary if one or more coronary arteries have developed severe atherosclerotic deposits that threaten to clog the arteries and to cause a heart attack. In order to avoid a heart attack, a coronary bypass operation is frequently performed. It surgically constructs a bypass around the atherosclerotic deposits in order to guarantee unrestricted blood flow to all parts of the heart muscle in those areas beyond the coronary deposits.

During a bypass operation, a vein is generally taken from the leg and re-implanted as a bypass blood vessel. Normally one end of the bypass is attached to the aorta and the other end to the coronary artery beyond the location narrowed by an ather-

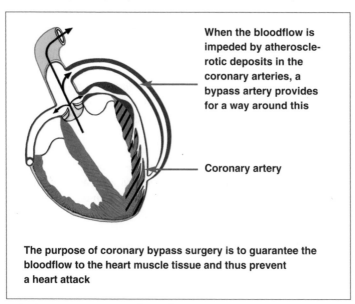

When the bloodflow is impeded by atherosclerotic deposits in the coronary arteries, a bypass artery provides for a way around this

Coronary artery

The purpose of coronary bypass surgery is to guarantee the bloodflow to the heart muscle tissue and thus prevent a heart attack

Why bypass surgery is performed

159

osclerotic deposit. Other bypass surgery procedures use smaller arteries in the vicinity of the heart to construct a bypass and to improve blood supply to the heart muscle.

I am often asked whether a coronary bypass operation can be avoided by following our vitamin program. As documented in this book, the operation can in many cases be postponed or cancelled. However, in other cases the atherosclerotic deposits have grown so far that a bypass operation is unavoidable. In any case, the decision can only be made together with your cardiologist. But even if a bypass operation has become inevitable, you should start immediately with Dr. Rath's Vitamin Program to improve the long-term success of this operation and to prevent further damage.

What Are the Main Problems After a Coronary Bypass Operation?

The overall success of a coronary artery bypass operation is threatened by two main problems:

- **Blood clots.** Blood clots can form in the bypass blood vessels, cutting off the blood flow. This complication normally occurs immediately after the operation. If untreated, this blood clot will completely cut off the blood flow through the bypass blood vessel and thereby make the previous operation ineffective.

- **Atherosclerotic deposits.** The greatest threat to the long-term success of a coronary bypass operation is the development of atherosclerotic deposits in the newly implanted bypass blood vessels. Even though the bypass blood vessel is generally a vein, the same lesions and cracks can develop as in the arteries if they are not protected by an optimum intake of vitamins and other essential nutrients. This triggers atherosclerotic deposits similar to those in the regular coronary arteries and, after several years, can require a second bypass operation.

The average time that passes between the first bypass operation of a patient and the second bypass surgery is about 10 years. The fact that a second bypass is the rule, and not the exception, shows that the causes of bypass atherosclerosis are insufficiently understood by conventional medicine.

On the following pages I have summarized the recent progress from the field of Cellular Medicine.

How Dr. Rath's Vitamin Program Improves the Long-Term Success of Coronary Bypass Surgery

There are several ways in which nutritional supplements help to maintain healthy bypass blood vessels and thereby improve the quality of life after bypass surgery.

• **Preventing blood clot formation in bypass blood vessels.** Vitamin C, vitamin E, and beta carotene have all been shown to help prevent the formation of blood clots. Vitamin C has also been shown to help dissolve already existing blood clots. Patients on Coumadin and other "blood thinners" should inform their doctors when starting on Dr. Rath's Vitamin Program so that additional tests for blood coagulation can be done and less blood-thinning medication may be prescribed.

• **Preventing atherosclerotic deposits in bypass blood vessels.** The vitamins and other essential nutrients recommended for the prevention and adjunct reversal of atherosclerotic deposits in coronary arteries are also beneficial for preventing the development of atherosclerotic deposits in bypass blood vessels. The most important among these essential nutrients are vitamin C, vitamin E, beta-carotene, and the amino acids lysine and proline.

If you are scheduled for a bypass operation, I recommend that you start with this vitamin program as soon as possible. In this way, you make sure that the cells of the heart, the blood ves-

1. Complication:

Blood Clot For mation in Bypass Vessels:

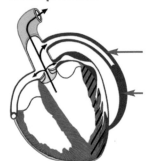

Coronary Bypass Blood Vessels

Blood Clot Blocking Blood Flow in Bypass

2. Complication:

New Deposits Develop in Bypass Grafts and Old Deposits in Coronary Arteries Continue to Grow

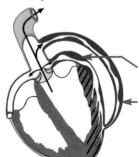

Old Deposits

New Deposits

Dr. Rath's Vitamin Program Can Improve Short-Term and Long-Term Success Rate After Coronary Bypass Surgery:

Nutrients Decreasing Risk for Blood Clotting:
- Vitamin C   • Beta-Carotene
- Vitamin E   • Arginine

Nutrients Decreasing Risk for New Deposits:
- Vitamin C   • Proline
- Lysine   • Antioxidants

Obstacles to the Long-Term Success of Coronary Bypass Surgery and How Dr. Rath's Vitamin Program Helps to Prevent Them

sels, and other body tissues already hold an optimum level of vitamins and other bioenergy molecules during and immediately after the operation. This is the best natural way to optimize the healing process (see also chapter on Surgery).

Following is a sample testimonial from a patient starting Dr. Rath's Vitamin Program after having undergone coronary bypass surgery:

Dear Dr. Rath:

I read your book about a year ago when I was told I had severe blockage of the coronary arteries, and I had a triple bypass operation. At that time I started following your cardiovascular vitamin program.

All of my checkups since my surgery have been outstanding. I attribute much of the good news to your program.

For a long time I have maintained an opinion that there was a better answer to heart disease than the standard American Medical Association medical approach. Thank you for finding the answer and making it available to all of us who need it.

Sincerely,
C.S.

You will find many more letters from coronary heart disease patients in the chapters on cardiovascular disease, angina pectoris and heart attacks.

Dr. Rath's Vitamin Program and Coronary Angioplasty

What Is a Coronary Angioplasty?

In contrast to coronary bypass surgery, coronary angioplasty is the "rotor rooter" approach to removing atherosclerotic deposits mechanically. This approach generally involves an inflatable balloon or, more recently, laser or scraping methods. Generally, a catheter is inserted into the leg artery and moved forward through the aorta until the catheter tip reaches the coronary artery close to the deposits. At this point, a balloon at the tip of the catheter is inflated with high pressure, thereby squeezing the atherosclerotic deposits flat against the wall of the arteries. In many cases, the blood flow through the coronary artery can be improved by this procedure.

All angioplasty procedures damage the inside of the coronary arteries, sometimes over a distance of several inches. It is, therefore, not surprising that the rate of complications of this procedure is sobering. In over 30% of cases, a restenosis occurs, leading to the clogging of the coronary artery within as short a time as six months.

The most important complication during the procedure is the rupturing of the wall of the coronary artery, requiring immediate bypass operation. Following the procedure, blood clots and small pieces of artery wall tissue can lead to a clogging of the coronary artery. Long-term complications include the overgrowth of scar tissue inside the coronary artery and the continued development of atherosclerotic deposits.

How Dr. Rath's Vitamin Program Can Help to Improve The Success Rate After Angioplasty

Dr. Rath's Vitamin Program can help patients scheduled for coronary angioplasty in different ways. In some cases, it can help decrease angina pectoris and other signs of coronary

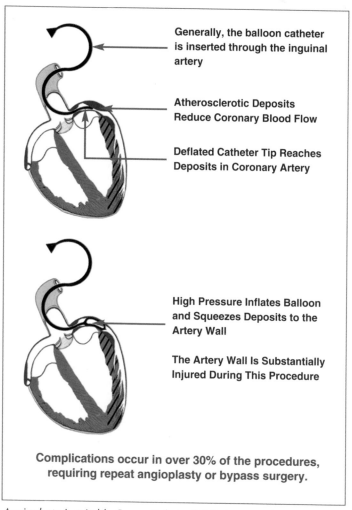

Generally, the balloon catheter is inserted through the inguinal artery

Atherosclerotic Deposits Reduce Coronary Blood Flow

Deflated Catheter Tip Reaches Deposits in Coronary Artery

High Pressure Inflates Balloon and Squeezes Deposits to the Artery Wall

The Artery Wall Is Substantially Injured During This Procedure

Complications occur in over 30% of the procedures, requiring repeat angioplasty or bypass surgery.

Angioplasty Inevitably Causes Substantial Damage to the Artery Wall

heart disease to an extent that your doctor will suggest postponement of the angioplasty procedure. In other cases, your doctor will advise you to carry out the procedure to minimize your risk of a heart attack. In any case, you should follow the advice of your doctor. At the same time, I recommend that you should start this vitamin program as soon as possible and inform your doctor about it. If you have already undergone coronary angioplasty, Dr. Rath's Vitamin Program can help you to improve the long-term success of this procedure.

- Vitamin C accelerates healing of the wounds in the coronary arteries caused by the angioplasty procedure.

- Lysine and proline also help in the re-formation of the artery wall and at the same time decrease the risk of fatty deposits.

- Vitamin E and vitamin C help control the overshooting formation of scar tissue from the uncontrolled growth of arterial wall muscle cells.

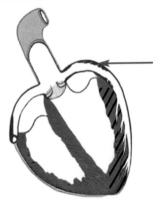

- **by Helping to Prevent the Formation of Blood Clots at the Site of the Injured Artery**

- **by Promoting the Healing of the Injured Artery Wall After Angioplasty**

The Following Essential Nutrients Can Improve the Long-Term Success of Coronary Angioplasty
- **Vitamin C**   • **Lysine**
- **Vitamin E**   • **Proline**

Dr. Rath's Vitamin Program Can Improve the Success Rate of Coronary Angioplasty

- Vitamin C, vitamin E, and beta-carotene decrease the risk of blood clot formation and provide important antioxidant protection.

Further Health Information Related to Dr. Rath's Vitamin Program and Angioplasty

Research and clinical studies have confirmed the important role of different components of Dr. Rath's Vitamin Program in decreasing the risk of clogging of coronary arteries after angioplasty:

Dr. DeMeio from Emory University in Atlanta, Georgia, U.S.A., studied patients with coronary heart disease who underwent coronary angioplasty. After this procedure, one group of the patients received 1,200 International Units (I.U.) of vitamin E as a nutritional supplement. The control group received no additional vitamin E. After four months, the patients who had received vitamin E showed a 15% decrease in the rate of coronary restenosis compared to those patients without vitamin E supplementation.

My colleague, Dr. Aleksandra Niedzwiecki, and her collaborators showed that vitamin C decreases the overgrowth of the smooth muscle cells of the artery wall, and thereby helps to control one of the most frequent factors responsible for the failure of angioplasty procedures. Animal experiments by Dr. Nunes and his colleagues confirmed these observations for vitamin C and vitamin E.

Dr. Rath's Vitamin Program contains a selection of essential nutrients that work synergistically in helping to improve the long-term success after coronary angioplasty. Of course, you can increase the amounts of specific vitamins, such as vitamin C and vitamin E, to further enhance this effect.

167

Following is a sample letter from an patient who started Dr. Rath's Vitamin Program after having had coronary angioplasty:

Dear Dr. Rath:

Your vitamin program has done so much to improve the quality of my life, healthwise, that I would like to share it with others. *I was 83 years old last February. I was having so much angina pain that my family doctor sent me to a cardiologist, who did an angioplasty. In the meantime my 78-year-old husband had triple by-pass followed by a stroke. I had to get better to take care of him, but I continued to have the same pains.* **A second cardiologist did angioplasty in August last year which did not help, so in September I had a double by-pass, needing a third.**

My son started me on your vitamin program. In January of this year I was still having angina, due to an artery they were unable to by-pass. **After 3 months I quit having pains, due to stress or strain or excitement and now, after six months, I feel great and do almost as much physically as I did 5 or 10 years ago.**

My husband, although hampered by his stroke, also enjoys better health with your cardiovascular health program.

Sincerely,
L.W.

More letters from coronary heart disease patients are documented in the previous chapters.

External and Inherited Cardiovascular Risk

9

Dr. Rath's Vitamin Program Helps to Reduce External and Inherited Cardiovascular Risk

- Unhealthy Diet

- Smoking

- Stress

- Hormonal Contraceptives

- Diuretic Medication

- Prescription Drugs

- Dialysis

- Surgery

- Inherited Cardiocascular Risk Factors

Unhealthy Diet

The basis of any natural cardiovascular health program is a healthy diet. For many generations, the diet of our ancestors shaped the metabolism of our bodies today. By understanding our ancestors' diet we have learned what is best for our bodies today. Their diet was rich in cereal, fruits, vegetables, and other plant nutrition high in fiber and vitamins. They ate considerably less fat and sugar than our diet today. Vice versa, the average diet in the industrialized countries imposes a heavy metabolic burden on our bodies. Certain inherited disorders put our bodies at further risk. Thus, it is good to know that many components of Dr. Rath's Vitamin Program have been shown to optimize our metabolism. This is particularly important for the metabolism of fat in our body. This vitamin program helps you to:

- Lower cholesterol production in the body
- Optimize the metabolism of fat molecules in cells
- Optimize the elimination of fat from the body
- Protect fat molecules from oxidation

It is important to understand that certain vitamins are literally used up in the degradation process of these fat molecules. For example, for every molecule of cholesterol, whether it is produced in the body or comes from the diet, our body uses up one molecule of vitamin C in an enzymatic reaction in the liver. In this way, high cholesterol and triglyceride levels can contribute to a chronic vitamin depletion of the body. Thus, it is important to understand that the increased cardiovascular risk is not primarily the result of too many fat molecules in the diet, but it comes from the systematic depletion of the vitamin reserves in our bodies from an overburdened fat metabolism. As a consequence of chronic vitamin depletion, the artery walls are weakened and cardiovascular disease develops.

Besides too much fat, there are other dangers in our diet. Residues from herbicides, pesticides, and chemical preservatives are present in essentially every meal we eat. These toxic substances have to be detoxified in our liver. Vitamin C and other components of Dr. Rath's Vitamin Program are essential cofactors for a rapid detoxification of these substances in our bodies.

My recommendation

Eat a prudent diet. Watch your body weight, and exercise regularly. A healthy diet is rich in plant nutrition and contains abundant vitamins and fiber substances, which also help to optimize digestion. Try to avoid too much fat and sweetened food. Above all, avoid chronic depletion of your body's vitamin reserves by following this vitamin program on a daily basis.

Smoking

While it is generally known that smoking dramatically increases the risk for cardiovascular disease, the underlying reason is unclear. In particular, the smoke from cigarettes contains millions of free radicals, those aggressive molecules that damage the cells of our blood vessels and other organs and accelerate the biological rusting. Free radicals and other toxic substances in cigarette smoke reach the blood stream from the lungs. These noxious substances can damage the blood vessel pipeline along its entire length of 60,000 miles. Now we understand why smokers have a specific form of atherosclerosis, which frequently starts in the body periphery, e.g., the toes, feet, and legs. In this case, atherosclerosis is not limited to the coronary arteries, but the damage also occurs in the small arteries and capillaries throughout the body. The "smoker foot" is proverbial and frequently toes, foot, or part of the leg must be amputated.

Dr. Rath's Vitamin Program contains numerous antioxidants, which are able to neutralize free radicals contained in the smoke, thereby helping to prevent damage to the artery wall and other body tissues.

My recommendation

If you still smoke, it is worth another effort to stop. Perhaps this chapter will help you become aware of how much damage you actually cause in your body by smoking. For smokers and ex-smokers, my recommendations are the same: Optimize your daily intake of natural antioxidants, preferably in the form of Dr. Rath's Vitamin Program.

Stress

Chronic physical and psychological stress increase the risk for cardiovascular disease. What is the underlying biochemical mechanism for this phenomenon? During physical or emotional stress, the body produces high amounts of the stress hormone adrenaline. For every molecule of adrenaline produced, the body needs a molecule of vitamin C as the catalyst. These vitamin C molecules are destroyed in these reactions. Thus, long-term physical or emotional stress can lead to a severe depletion of the body's reservoir of vitamin C. If vitamin C is not supplemented in the diet, the cardiovascular system is weakened, and atherosclerosis develops.

These facts also explain why spouses frequently die soon after one another. The loss of a partner results in long-term emotional stress and a fast vitamin depletion of the body, thereby increasing the risk for a heart attack. We have to understand that it is not the emotional stress itself that causes the heart attack, but the biochemical consequence, the depletion of the vitamin reserves in the body.

My recommendation

Try to find time to relax. Schedule hours and days to relax just as you schedule your professional appointments. With severe emotional problems you may also benefit from a professional consultation. Irrespective of these steps, make sure that you supplement your body's reservoir of vitamins and other components of this vitamin program.

Hormonal Contraceptives

Several studies show that women taking hormonal contraceptives ("The Pill") significantly increase their risk for cardiovascular disease. What is the biochemical basis for this phenomenon? In 1972, Dr. Briggs reported in the scientific journal, *Nature,* that women taking hormonal contraceptives had significantly lower vitamin C blood levels than normal. In another study, Dr. Rivers confirmed these results and concluded that the vitamin C depletion is associated with the estrogen hormone. The fact is that long-term use of hormone contraceptives decreases the body pool of vitamin C and also of other essential nutrients. Thus, it is not the birth control pill itself that increases the risk for cardiovascular disease, but the associated depletion of the vitamin body pool, leading to a weakening of the blood vessel wall.

My recommendation

If you are taking hormonal birth control pills, or if you have taken them in the past, I recommend that you start following Dr. Rath's Vitamin Program to re-supplement your body's vitamin pool and to prevent its future depletion.

Diuretic Drugs

Taking diuretic drugs can significantly increase your risk for cardiovascular disease. Diuretics flush not only water from the body, but also water soluble vitamins and other essential nutrients. I described this mechanism in detail in the chapter on Heart Failure. The importance of a regular supplementation of these vitamins and other essential nutrients in patients taking diuretics cannot be over emphasized.

Other Prescription Drugs

Besides diuretics, the other prescription drugs currently taken by millions of people lead to a gradual depletion of vitamins and other components of Dr. Rath's Vitamin in the body. Drugs are generally synthetic, non-natural substances, which we take up in our body. Different drugs can contribute in different ways to the depletion of the body's vitamin reserves:

All synthetic drugs have to be "detoxified" by the liver in order to be eliminated from the body. This "detoxification" process requires vitamin C and also other components of Dr. Rath's Vitamin Program as cofactors. Many of these essential nutrients are used up in biocatalytic reactions during this "detoxification" process. Thus, long-term use of many synthetic prescription drugs leads to a chronic vitamin depletion of the body and, thereby, to the onset of cardiovascular disease.

Another way in which certain prescription drugs such as the cholesterol-lowering agent Cholestyramine, contribute to vitamin depletion is their binding to vitamins in the digestive tract. This prevents optimum absorption of vitamins from the digestive tract into the bloodstream and the body.

Prescription drugs can also deplete the body's reservoir of certain essential nutrients by interfering with the natural production of these essential nutrients in the body. Lovastatin, Pravastatin, and other cholesterol-lowering drugs of the "statin"-group inhibit the production of cholesterol in the cells of the body. Unfortunately, they also decrease the production rate of important natural molecules in the body, such as coenzyme Q10 (ubiquinone). Professor Folkers, from the University of Texas in Austin, reported that heart failure patients with low baseline coenzyme Q10 levels can experience life-threatening cardiovascular complications when taking these cholesterol-lowering drugs because of a further decrease of coenzyme Q10 in the body.

My recommendation

If you are taking any prescription drug, I recommend that you also begin Dr. Rath's Vitamin Program. Play it safe. Follow the recommendations of this book, and inform your doctor about it.

Dialysis

Several investigations have shown that patients undergoing long-term dialysis have an increased risk of cardiovascular disease. This is not surprising, since dialysis eliminates not only the body's waste products from the blood circulation, but also many vitamins and other essential nutrients. If these essential nutrients are not resupplemented, chronic dialysis will lead to a gradual depletion of vitamins and other essential nutrients throughout the body, thereby triggering atherosclerosis and cardiovascular disease.

My recommendation

If you are undergoing dialysis, you should immediately start following Dr. Rath's Vitamin Program. If you know a dialysis patient, please make sure that you hand over the information from this book; you could help prolong a life.

Surgery

Patients undergoing an operation should make sure that the cells of their bodies are optimally supplied with vitamins and other components of Dr. Rath's Vitamin Program. This program can help you before, during, and after the operation.

Dr. Raths Vitamin Program replaces the essential nutrients depleted during the physical and emotional stress of an operation. Each operation results in extraordinary physical and psychological stress for the patient. I have already explained the direct connection between stress and vitamin depletion. Preparation for the operation, the operation itself, and the healing phase after an operation frequently result in high stress for several weeks, and can lead to a serious vitamin depletion of your body at a time of greatest need.

Dr. Rath's Vitamin Program accelerates wound healing. Each operation is associated with damage to body tissue to a lesser or greater extent. The speed at which the operation wound heals is directly related to the rate at which collagen and other connective tissue molecules are formed and heal the wound. Vitamin C and other components of Dr. Rath's Vitamin Program are your best natural options for optimizing the production of collagen molecules and to speed up the healing phase after an operation.

Dr. Rath's Vitamin Program protects from oxidative damage during operations. A variety of operation procedures require an extra-corporeal circulation during the operation itself. During a bypass operation, for example, the heartbeat is artificially stopped and the blood circulation is maintained by a heart-lung machine. During this extra-corporeal circulation, the patient's blood is artificially enriched with oxygen. It is a well known fact that high concentrations of oxygen can lead to tissue damage of the artery walls and other body tissues (reperfusion injury). Dr. Rath's Vitamin Program is rich in antioxidants and can minimize the risks of oxidative damage during an operation.

These are the reasons why every patient should start on Dr. Rath's Vitamin Program as soon as possible before an operation. Inform your doctor about it and follow Dr. Rath's Vitamin Program while in the hospital. If your doctors are still reluctant to approve this program, you can tell them that Harvard Medical School and other leading medical universities are now routinely recommending vitamin supplementation to their patients undergoing surgery.

The following table summarizes some of the studies underlining the importance of vitamins and other ingredients of Dr. Rath's Vitamin Program in decreasing different external risk factors for cardiovascular disease:

External Risk Factors Studied	References
Blood Fats	Ginter, Harwood, Sokoloff
Smoking	Chow, Halliwell, Lehr, Riemersma
Stress	Levine
"The Pill"	Briggs, Rivers
Dialysis	Blumberg
Prescription Drugs	Halliwell, Clemetson

Inherited Risk Factors for Cardiovascular Disease

I am frequently asked whether this vitamin program can also help decrease the risk of inherited risk factors. In many cases, the answer is "yes." Besides the external risk factors discussed in the previous section, the inherited, or genetic, risk is the second large group of cardiovascular risk factors. We have all heard the sentence, "Heart disease runs in our family." Members of these families frequently die in the fourth or fifth decade of their lives. The causes of these early deaths are, at least in part, caused by abnormal genes (molecules of inheritance), which are passed on from generation to generation in that family. Earlier in this book I described two of the most frequent genetic risk factors – inherited disorders of fat metabolism (high cholesterol, hypercholesterolemia) and inherited disorders of sugar metabolism (diabetes).

What is important to understand is that this genetic risk is no death sentence for anybody. The genetic deficiency generally results in an impaired metabolic function at one location or another in our cellular software program (see first chapters of this book). In most cases this genetic impairment can be compensated for by an increased intake of essential nutrients. As we already know, vitamins and other essential nutrients are cellular energy carriers and they are able to speed-up biochemical reactions that are impaired.

It is therefore no surprise that vitamins and other essential nutrients have already been shown to have profound health benefits in patients with genetic disorders.

The following table provides a list of inherited disorders. Patients with these disorders can benefit from following Dr. Rath's vitamin program.

If you know anyone with one of the following inherited diseases please introduce this book and this information to them. As you can see from the history of the Alzheimer and lupus erythematosus patients at the end of this section, these patients can only win by immediately starting Dr. Rath's Vitamin Program, a natural and safe approach to these health conditions. This is even more important considering the fact that conventional medicine has no answers to these serious health problems.

Patients with the Following Inherited Disorders Should Start on Dr. Rath's Vitamin Program

– *Diabetes*
– *Homocystinuria*
– *Alzheimer's Disease*
– *Neurofibromatosis*
– *Cystic Fibrosis*
– *Lupus Erythematosus*
– *Scleroderma*
– *Muscular Dystrophy*
– *Parkinson's Disease*
– *Multiple Sclerosis*
– *Addison's disease*
– *Amyloidosis*
– *Morbus Cushing*
– *Down's Syndrome*
– *Rheumatoid Arthritis*
– *Connective Tissue Disorders*

How does Dr. Rath's Vitamin Program decrease the cardiovascular risk associated with these inherited risk factors? Let's take diabetes, for example. With this disease, a genetic defect results in too little production or cellular availability of the insulin hormone. The clinical consequences are discussed in detail in the diabetes chapter. Although Dr. Rath's Vitamin Program cannot repair the defective gene, it can help prevent triggering the diabetic glucose imbalance, as well as development of diabetic cardiovascular complications. In the adjacent figure, the defective gene is symbolized as a time bomb. This nutritional supplement program cannot make this time bomb disappear; however, it can contribute to defusing it and thereby prevent an explosion in the form of a metabolic imbalance or the initiation of disease symptoms. As documented in this book for diabetes, cholesterol disorders, Alzheimer's Disease, Lupus Erythematosus and other conditions, Dr. Rath's Vitamin Program is the first effective therapeutic approaches to reduce the risk from inherited disorders particularly the development of cardiovascular complications.

The adjacent figure summarizes the main factors contributing to your personal cardiovascular risk. Inherited risk factors plus external risk factors determine your overall risk for cardiovascular disease by gradually depleting your body's reservoir of essential nutrients. Most internal and external risk factors are effectively neutralized by an optimum intake of vitamins and other essential nutrients. You can minimize your cardiovascular risk by two distinct measures: increasing your daily intake of essential nutrients and minimizing your external risk factors such as smoking and an unhealthy diet.

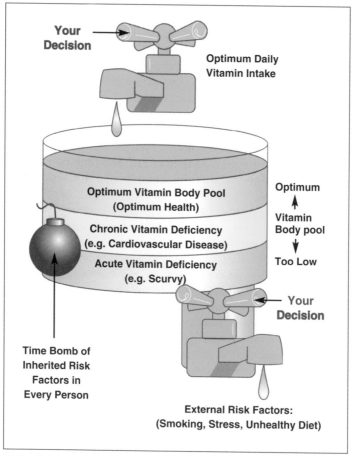

Maintaining an Optimum Body Pool of Essential Nutrients Is the Key to Optimum Health

Dr. Rath's Vitamin Program Can Help Alzheimer Patients

Alzheimer's disease is a degenerative disease that leads to the gradual impairment of brain function. Conventional medicine has no therapy for this serious health problem.

Dear Dr. Rath:

My father, who is 84, has Alzheimer's Disease. *About two months ago his caregivers attended an Alzheimer's seminar at a nursing home there. The seminar reported that some patients had been put on vitamin supplements, which had resulted in improved memory for several patients. We compared ingredients and decided that your cardiovascular vitamin program offered more than what was used at the nursing home.*

My father has been on this program for two months and we cannot believe the improvement. His short-term memory is improving and we can carry on conversations with him again. He is even showing some problem solving capabilities again. *I know these improvements are not measurable from a "pure scientific perspective" but to us it's a blessing to see improvement rather than just deterioration from this terrible disease*

On behalf o my father and our family, thank you for your cardio-vascular health program.

Yours truly,
D.C.

Dr. Rath's Vitamin Program Can Help Patients With Lupus Erythematosus

Lupus erythematosus is a so-called "autoimmune disease"disease. It can lead to inflammation, hardening impairment and, eventually, failure of just about any organ in the body. Conventional medicine has no therapy for this serious health problem.

Dear Dr. Rath:

*I was very impressed with your research and particularly interested in your theory of many degenerative diseases being related to long term nutritional deficiencies, because **my sister suffered so much from lupus erythematosus disease.** She has been diagnosed with it in 1973 and since that time she has been hospitalized more times than I can remember and has **suffered from phlebitis (inflammation of the veins) shingles, ulcerative colitis (inflammation of the bowel), and her vision has steadily deteriorated.***

*She is 44 years old, married and mother of 3 children. In 1989 a routine PAP-smear showed severe inflammation and pre-cancerous tissue. Her doctors tried to treat this condition with drugs first, and later with "laser burn" treatments. This reduced the number of cells somewhat but did not end the problem. A subsequent PAP-smear showed that the number of cells was increasing and they performed a complete hysterectomy. **Even after the hysterectomy she still had severe inflammation and a large number of pre-cancerous cells.***

Other treatments had been also ineffective. Basically, her doctors didn't know what else to try.

***In November of 1994 she began following your vitamin program together with a fiber drink.** Even though she was somewhat skeptical, she felt that she had nothing to lose. In July of 1995 (after 8 months on your program) she had another pap-smear test taken. What a tremendous feeling of joy she must have felt when her*

---

*doctor told her that her PAP smear came back **perfectly normal with no inflammation and no pre-cancerous cells.** Her doctor asked her what she was doing differently, She told her doctor about the vitamin program. Her doctor replied she didn't understand it, but couldn't argue with success.*

*There was also other benefit. In July 1995 her ophthalmologist examined her eyes. The first thing he asked was: "What have you been doing differently since your previous check up?" **He said her eyes were "healthier" inside than he had ever seen them during the two and a half years he'd been treating her.***

Also, my sister is now able to limit her prednisone (anti-inflammatory medication) to the smallest dosage during the past 22 years. Thank you for your research and for your efforts to spread the word of your breakthrough discovery.

Sincerely,
S.S.

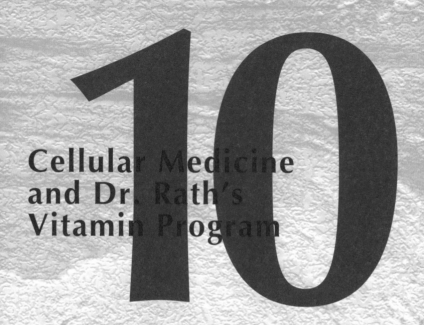

10

Cellular Medicine and Dr. Rath's Vitamin Program

The components of Dr. Rath's Vitamin Program

Dr. Rath's Vitamin Program as Bioenergy Source

Cellular Medicine

Scientific Facts About the Ingredients of Dr. Rath's Vitamin Program

Questions and Answers About Dr. Rath's Vitamin Program

Dr. Rath's Vitamin Program as Bioenergy Source

The components of Dr. Rath's Vitamin Program are an essential part of the biological fuel we have to provide regularly to our bodies. The other biological fuels are well known: air (oxygen), water, regular nutrition (composed of proteins, fats, and carbohydrates). There is a distinct characteristic setting vitamins apart from air, water, and food: a lack of vitamins and other essential nutrients does not give any alarm signs. Oxygen deficiency, for example, leads within minutes to the alarm sign of suffocation. Water deficiency's alarm sign is "thirst." Lack of food causes hunger.

In contrast, a deficiency of vitamins and other essential nutrients, the carriers of energy, do not give any alarm signs in the body. The first sign of a vitamin deficiency is the outbreak of a disease. A total depletion of vitamins, such as that in scurvy, leads to death within months. Since we all get small amounts of vitamins and other essential nutrients, we generally do not suffer from a total depletion.

Most of us, however, suffer from a chronic deficiency of vitamins and other essential nutrients. Since deficiencies of these essential nutrients do not give any immediate alarm signs, they continue to be unrecognized and masked for many years. In many cases, the first sign of chronic vitamin deficiency is a heart attack or the outbreak of another disease. Thus, since our body does not give us any alarm signs, the best way we can avoid deficiencies in cellular energy is an optimum daily supplementation of the different components of Dr. Rath's Vitamin Program.

Oxygen	Water

Regular Food	Essential Nutrients
· Sugar	· Vitamins
· Fat	· Amino Acids
· Protein	· Minerals
	· Trace elements

Missing Life Essentials	Early Alarm Signs	Death Occurs Within
No Oxygen	— Suffocation →	Minutes
No Water	— Thirst →	Days
No Food	— Hunger →	Weeks
Zero Vitamins	— **None !** →	Months (e.g. Scurvy)
Vitamin Defciency	— **None !** →	Many Years (e.g. Heart Attack)

Bioenergy sources for the body

Cellular Medicine

This book introduces the era of Cellular Medicine. This new era of human health is based on a new understanding of health and disease: Health and disease of our body and all its organs is determined by the function of millions of cells. Optimum functioning of these building stones of life means health; in contrast, cellular malfunction causes disease.

The primary, and by far the most frequent, cause of malfunctioning of cells is a chronic deficiency of essential nutrients, in particular of vitamins, amino acids, minerals, and trace elements. These essential nutrients are needed for a multitude of biochemical reactions and other cellular functions in every single cell of our body. Chronic deficiencies of one or more of these essential nutrients, therefore, must lead to cellular malfunctioning and to disease.

Cellular medicine can also explain why cardiovascular disease is still the number one cause of death. The heart and the circulatory system are the most active organs of our body because of their continuous pumping function. Because of the high mechanical demands, the cells of the cardiovascular system have a high rate of consumption of vitamins and other essential nutrients.

Finally, Cellular Medicine identifies an optimum daily intake of vitamins and other essential nutrients as a basic preventive and therapeutic measure for cardiovascular diseases as well as many other health conditions. Towards this aim, Dr. Rath's Vitamin Program provides the most important essential nutrients.

The Principles of Cellular Medicine

I.   Health and disease are determined on the level of millions of cells which compose our body and its organs.

II. Vitamins and other essential nutrients are needed for thousands of biochemical reactions in each cell. Chronic deficiency of these vitamins and other essential nutrients is the most frequent cause of malfunction of millions of body cells and the primary cause of cardiovascular disease and other diseases.

III. Cardiovascular diseases are the most frequent diseases because cardiovascular cells consume vitamins and other essential nutrients at a high rate due to the mechanical stress on the heart and the blood vessel wall from the heartbeat and the pulse wave.

IV. Optimum dietary supplementation of vitamins and other essential nutrients is the key to prevention and effective treatment of cardiovascular disease, as well as other chronic health conditions.

The Main Function of Dr. Rath's Vitamin Program: Supply of Cellular Energy

Most carriers of bioenergy in cellular metabolism use components of Dr. Rath's Vitamin Program. The adjacent figure summarizes important details:

• **Acetyl-Coenzyme A (Acetyl-CoA),** the central molecule of cellular metabolism, is indispensable for processing of all components of food (carbohydrates, proteins, fats) and for their conversion into bioenergy. Vitamin B5 (pantothenic acid) is a structural component of this key molecule. A deficiency of vitamin B5 leads to decreased Acetyl-CoenzymA levels and to a metabolic "jam." This can result in increased blood levels of cholesterol and other blood fats. Optimum supplementation of vitamin B5 corrects this "jam" and improves the production of cellular energy.

• **Vitamin B3 (nicotinic acid)** is the energy transport molecule of one of the most important cellular energy carriers, called nicotinamide-adenine-dinucleotide (NAD). Vitamin C provides the bioenergy to the NAD transport molecules by adding hydrogen atoms (-H) and thereby, biological energy. The energy-rich shuttle molecules NAD-H provide energy for thousands of cellular reactions. Sufficient supply of vitamin B3 and vitamin C is indispensable for optimum cellular energy.

• **Vitamin B2 (riboflavin)** and vitamin C cooperate in a similar way within each cell as a bioenergy shuttle. Vitamin B2 is a structural component of the energy transport molecule flavin-adenine-dinucleotide (FAD) and vitamin C provides bioenergy for the activation of millions of bioenergy-rich FAD molecules.

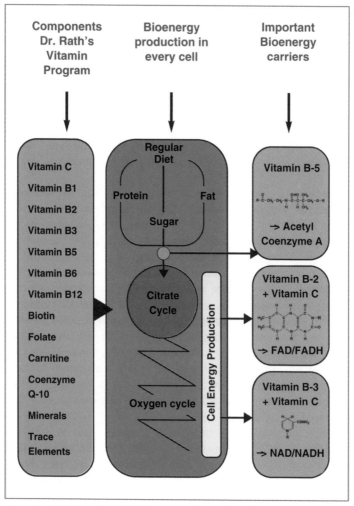

Essential Nutrients Provide Bioenergy for Each Cell

Scientific Facts About the Ingredients of Dr. Rath's Vitamin Program

The worldwide success of Dr. Rath's Vitamin Program is due to the fact that this natural program is scientifically based. The exact biochemical composition and many biological functions of the ingredients of Dr. Rath's Vitamin Program are known. Thus, the health benefits of this vitamin program are reproducible and millions of people around the world can benefit from them.

For each component of Dr. Rath's Vitamin Program there are numerous scientific studies substantiating their great importance for human health. The following pages summarize the comprehensive knowledge about the importance of each of the ingredients of this essential nutrient program. Many of these biochemical functions and health benefits are already contained in the leading textbooks in biology and biochemistry. Unfortunately, many textbooks in Medicine are still lacking this life-saving knowledge. The leading textbook for cardiologists, Eugene Braunwald's *"The Heart – Textbook of Cardiovascular Medicine"* does not mention vitamin C one single time on 2,000 pages of teaching material for future cardiologists. Now it turns out that this vitamin is the single most important reason why animals don't get heart attacks – but people do.

It is the intention of this book to bring about the necessary transformation in medicine in a constructive way. The following pages contain the most important facts about the components of Dr. Rath's Vitamin Program. These pages also help an increasing number of physicians and health professionals to implement the principles of Cellular Medicine in their daily practice.

The Scientific Basis of Dr. Rath's Vitamin Program

The real power of Dr. Rath's Vitamin Program becomes obvious if we have a close look at the different ingredients and what medical science tells us about their importance for our health.

Vitamins

Vitamin C
Vitamin C is the key nutrient for the stability of our blood vessels, our heart, and all other organs of our body. Without vitamin C our body would literally collapse and dissolve, as in scurvy.

Vitamin C is responsible for an optimum production and function of collagen, elastin and other connective tissue molecules that give stability to the blood vessel walls and to our body.
Vitamin C is important for fast wound healing throughout our body, including the healing of millions of tiny wounds and lesions at the inside of our blood vessel walls.

Vitamin C is the most important antioxidant of the body. Optimum amounts of vitamin C protect the cardiovascular system and the body effectively against biological rusting.

Vitamin C is also a cofactor for a series of biological catalysts (enzymes) which are important for an improved metabolism of cholesterol, triglycerides and other risk factors. This helps to decrease the risk for cardiovascular disease.

Vitamin C is an important energy molecule to recharge energy carriers inside the cells.

Vitamin E
Vitamin E is the most important fat soluble antioxidant vitamin. It protects particularly the membranes of the cells in our car-

diovascular system and our body against attacks from free radicals and against oxidative damage.

Vitamin E is enriched in low-density lipoproteins (LDL) and other cholesterol and fat transporting particles. Taken in optimum amounts, vitamin E can prevent these fat particles from oxidation (biological rusting) and from damaging the inside of the blood vessel walls.

Vitamin E was shown to render the platelets in our blood circulation less sticky, thereby keeping our blood thin and decreasing the risk from blood clotting.

Beta-Carotene

Beta-Carotene is also called pro-vitamin A and is another important fat soluble antioxidant vitamin. Like vitamin E, it is transported primarily in lipoprotein particles in our bloodstream to millions of body cells. Like vitamin E, beta-carotene protects these fat particles from rusting and from becoming damaging to the cardiovascular system. Considering these scientific facts, it is not surprising that vitamin C, vitamin E, and beta carotene are documented in a rapidly growing number of clinical studies as powerful protective agents against cardiovascular disease.

Similar to vitamin E, beta-carotene has been shown to decrease the risk from blood clotting.

Vitamin B-1 (Thiamine)

Thiamine functions as the cofactor for an important biocatalyst called pyrophosphate. This catalyst is involved in phosphate metabolism in our cells, another key energy source to optimize millions of reactions in our cardiovascular cells and our body.

Vitamin B-2 (Riboflavin)

Riboflavin is the cofactor for flavin-adenine-dinucleotide (FAD) one of the most important carrier molecules of cellular energy inside the tiny energy centers (power plants) of all cells.

Vitamin B-3 (Niacin, Niacinamide)

Niacin is an important nutrient essential as the cofactor for nicotinamide-adenine-dinucleotide (NAD) and related energy carrier molecules. This energy carrier molecule is one of the most important energy transport systems in our entire body. Millions of these carriers are created and recharged (by vitamin C) inside the cellular energy centers of our cardiovascular system and our body. Cell life and life in general would not be possible without this energy carrier.

Vitamin B-5 (Pantothenate)

Pantothenate is the cofactor for coenzyme A, the central fuel molecule in the metabolism of our heart cells, our blood vessel cells and all other cells. The metabolism of carbohydrates, proteins and fats inside each cell all lead into one single molecule, acetyl coenzyme A. This molecule is the key molecule that helps to convert all food into cell energy. This important molecule is actually composed in part of vitamin B-5, and the importance of supplementing this vitamin is evident. Again, cell life would not be possible without this vitamin.

Vitamin B-6 (Pyridoxine)

Vitamin B-6 is the cofactor for pyridoxal phosphate, an important co-factor for the metabolism of amino acids and proteins in our cardiovascular cells and our body.

Vitamin B-6 is needed in the production of red blood cells, the carriers of oxygen to the cells of our cardiovascular system and all other cells of our body.

Vitamin B-6 is also essential for optimum structure and function of collagen fibers.

Vitamin B-12

Vitamin B-12 is needed for a proper metabolism of fatty acids and certain amino acids in the cells of our body.

Vitamin B-12 is also required for the production of red blood cells. A severe deficiency of vitamin B-12 can cause a disease called pernicious anemia, which is characterized by an insufficient production of blood cells.

Folate

Folate is a very important nutrient for the production of red blood cells and for oxygen supply.

The last three vitamins are good examples of how these bioenergy molecules work together like an orchestra. Without proper oxygen transport to all the cells, their function would be impaired, no matter how much of the other vitamins you take. It is therefore important to supplement your diet as completely as possible with the right essential nutrients in the right amounts.

Biotin

Biotin is needed in the metabolism of carbohydrates, fats and proteins.

Vitamin D

Vitamin D is essential for optimum calcium and phosphate metabolism in the body.

Vitamin D is indispensable for bone formation, growth, and stability of our skeleton. Over centuries, vitamin D deficiency was a frequent children's disease, causing retarded growth and malformation. Even today, milk is frequently supplemented with this vitamin.

In our body vitamin D can also be synthesized from cholesterol molecules by the action of light.

In connection with cardiovascular disease, Vitamin D is essential for optimum calcium metabolism in the artery walls, including the removal of calcium from atherosclerotic deposits.

Minerals

Minerals are important essential nutrients. Calcium, magnesium, and potassium are the most important among them. Minerals are needed for a multitude of catalytic reactions in each cell of our body.

Calcium

Calcium is important for the proper contraction of muscle cells, including millions of heart muscle cells.

Calcium is needed for the conduction of nerve impulses and therefore for optimum heartbeat.

Calcium is also needed for the proper biological communication among the cells of the cardiovascular system and most other cells, as well as for many other biological functions.

Magnesium

Magnesium is nature's calcium antagonist, and its benefit for the cardiovascular system is similar to the calcium antagonist drugs that are prescribed, except that magnesium is produced by nature itself.

Clinical studies have shown that magnesium is particularly important for helping to normalize elevated blood pressure; moreover, it can help normalize irregular heartbeat.

Trace Elements

The trace elements zinc, manganese, copper, selenium, chromium, molybdenum are also important essential nutrients. Most of them are metals needed as catalysts for thousands of reactions in the metabolism of cells. They are needed only in very tiny amounts – less than a tenth of a thousandth of a gram. Selenium is also a very important antioxidant.

Amino Acids

Amino acids are the building blocks of proteins. Most of the amino acids in our body derive from regular food and from the breakdown of its protein content. Many amino acids can be synthesized in our body when needed; these amino acids are called "non-essential" amino acids. Those amino acids which the body can not synthesize are called "essential" amino acids.

Interestingly, there is now important scientific evidence that even though the body can produce certain amino acids, the amount produced may not be enough to maintain proper health. A good example is the amino acid proline.

Proline
The amino acid proline is a major building block of the stability proteins collagen and elastin. One fourth to one third of the collagen reinforcement rods, for example, are made up of proline. It is easy to understand how important it is for the optimum stability of our blood vessels and our body in general to get an optimum amount of proline in our diet.

Proline is also very important in the process of reversing atherosclerotic deposits. As described in this book in detail, cholesterol-carrying fat globules (lipoproteins) are attached to the inside of the blood vessel wall via biological adhesive tapes. Proline is a formidable "Teflon" agent, which can neutralize the stickiness of these fat globules. The therapeutic effect is two-fold. First, proline helps to prevent the further build-up of atherosclerotic deposits; second, proline helps to release already deposited fat globules from the blood vessel wall into the blood stream. When many fat globules are released from the plaques in the artery walls, the deposit size decreases, leading to a reversal of cardiovascular disease.

Proline can be synthesized by the body, but the amounts synthesized are frequently too little, particularly in patients with an increased risk for cardiovascular disease.

Lysine
As opposed to proline, lysine is an essential amino acid, which means that the body cannot synthesize this amino acid at all. A daily supplementation of this amino acid is therefore critical. Lysine, like proline, is an important building block of collagen and of other stability molecules and its intake helps to stabilize the blood vessels and the other organs in the body.

The combined intake of lysine and proline with vitamin C is of particular importance for optimum stability of body tissue. For optimum strength of the collagen molecules, its building blocks lysine and proline need to be biochemically modified to hydroxy-lysine and hydroxy-proline. Vitamin C is the most effective biocatalyst to accomplish this "hydroxylation" reaction, thereby providing optimum strenth to the connective tissue.

Lysine is another "Teflon" agent, which can help release deposited fat globules from the blood vessel deposits. People with existing cardiovascular disease may increase their daily intake of lysine and proline to several grams in addition to the basic program recommended in this book.

Lysine is also the precursor for the amino acid carnitine. The conversion from lysine into carnitine requires the presence of vitamin C as a biocatalyst. This is another reason why the combination of lysine with vitamin C is essential.

Arginine
Arginine has many functions in the human body. In connection with the cardiovascular system, one function is of particular importance. The amino acid arginine can split off a small molecule called nitric oxide. This tiny part of the former arginine molecule has a powerful role in maintaining cardiovascular health. Nitric oxide relaxes the blood vessel walls and thereby helps to normalize high blood pressure. In addition, nitric oxide helps to decrease the stickiness of platelets and thereby has an anti-clogging effect.

Carnitine
Carnitine is an extremely important amino acid and essential nutrient. It is needed for the proper conversion of fat into energy. Carnitine functions like a shuttle between the cell factory and the energy compartment within each cell. It transports energy molecules in and out of these cellular power plants. This mechanism is particularly important for all muscle cells,

including those of the heart. For the constantly pumping heart muscle, carnitine is one of the most critical cell fuels. Thus, it is not surprising that many clinical studies have documented the great value of carnitine supplementation in improving the pumping function and the performance of the heart.

Carnitine also benefits the electrical cells of the heart, and its supplementation has been shown to help normalize different forms of irregular heartbeat.

Cysteine

Cysteine is another important amino acid with many important functions in our body. The cardiovascular system benefits particularly from a supplementation with this amino acid because cysteine is a building block of glutathione, one of the most important antioxidants produced in the body. Among others, glutathione protects the inside of the blood vessel walls from free radical and other damage.

OTHER IMPORTANT INGREDIENTS

Coenzyme Q-10

Coenzyme Q-10 is a very important essential nutrient. It is also known as ubiquinone. Coenzyme Q-10 functions as an extremely important catalyst for the energy center of each cell. Because of its high work load, the heart muscle cells have a particularly high demand for Coenzyme Q-10. In patients with insufficient pumping function of the heart, this essential nutrient is frequently deficient. An irrefutable number of clinical studies have documented the great value of Coenzyme Q-10 in the treatment of heart failure and for optimum heart performance.

Inositol

Inositol is essential for sugar and fat metabolism in the cells of our body.

Inositol is also important for the biological communication process between the cells and organs of our body. Hormones such as insulin, and other molecules, are signals from outside the cell. If a hormone docks to a cell, it wishes to transmit information to this cell. Inositol is part of the proper reading mechanism of this information through the cell membrane. Thus, inositol is part of the proper biological communication process, which, in turn, is critical for optimum cardiovascular health.

Pycnogenols

Pycnogenols refers to a group of bioflavonoids (pro-antho-cyanidins) with remarkable properties. In the cardiovascular system, pycnogenols have several important functions:

– Pycnogenols are powerful antioxidants that work together with vitamin C and vitamin E in preventing damage to the cardiovascular system by free radicals.

– Together with vitamin C, pycnogenols have a particular value in stabilizing the blood vessel walls, including the capillaries. Pycnogenols have been shown to bind to elastin, the most important elasticity molecule, and protect elastin molecules against enzymatic degradation.

Biological Targets for Prevention of Cardiovascular Disease

Conventional Medicine

Dr. Rath's Vitamin Program stands comparison with any other preventive cardiovascular approaches. Preventive approaches by conventional medicine focus on cholesterol-lowering, reduction of other risk factors, and life style changes. Cardiovascular prevention programs based on lifestyle changes alone are limited by the fact that they lack key targets of cardiovascular health such as optimum antioxidant protection, optimum vascular stability and repair, as well as optimum resupplementation of cell fuels.

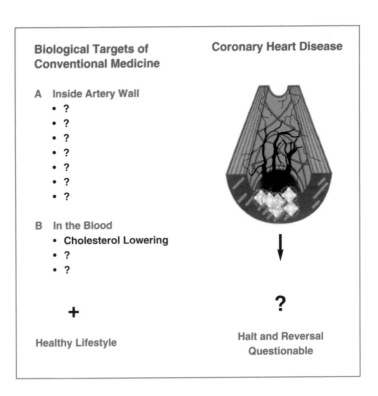

Cellular Medicine

In contrast, Dr. Rath's Vitamin Program has defined biological targets. No other preventive health program currently available anywhere targets the main problems of cardiovascular disease in such a direct and comprehensive way. Vascular wall stability is optimized, vascular healing processes are induced, antioxidant and "Teflon" protection is provided. The most important biological targets of this natural cardiovascular health program are summarized in the figure below.

Biological Targets of Cellular Medicine

Coronary Heart Disease

A Inside Artery Wall
- **Stability of Artery Wall**
- **Healing of Wall**
- **Reversal of Deposits**
- **"Teflon" Protection**
- **Antioxidant Protection**
- **Bioenergy for Cells**
- **Relaxation of Wall**

B In the Blood
- **Lowering of Risk Factors**
- **Optimum Blood Viscosity**
- **Healthy Blood Cells**

Healthy Lifestyle

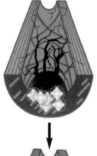

Natural Reversal Is Possible!

205

Dr. Rath's Vitamin Program Compared to Conventional Therapies

Effectiveness

Conventional therapy is generally limited to the treatment of cardiovascular *symptoms* and one at a time. Since most heart disease patients have many cardiovascular problems at the same time, they frequently are prescribed several medications. In contrast, Dr. Rath's Vitamin Program corrects the underlying causes of the disease. It provides the cell fuels for millions of cells, allowing for correction of impaired cellular function in different compartments of the cardiovascular system at the same time. With this figure I would also like to encourage my colleagues in medicine to use causal therapies wherever possible.

Conventional Medicine Primarily Treats Symptoms

Medication Type	Treatment of Symptoms	
Nitrate Group	➤ Angina Pectoris	(Symptoms)
Antiarrhythmic Drugs	➤ Arrhythmia	(Symptoms)
Betablocker Group	➤ High Blood Pressure	(Symptoms)
Diuretic Group	➤ Heart Failure	(Symptoms)

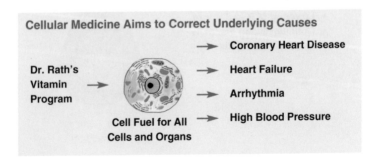

Cellular Medicine Aims to Correct Underlying Causes

Dr. Rath's Vitamin Program → Cell Fuel for All Cells and Organs →
- Coronary Heart Disease
- Heart Failure
- Arrhythmia
- High Blood Pressure

Safety

Another important advantage of Dr. Rath's Vitamin Program compared to conventional drug therapies is that it is safe, and undesired side effects are unknown. Dr. A. Bendich recently summarized the safety aspects of vitamins in a review for the *New York Academy of Sciences*. She found that all rumors about side effects of vitamins are unsubstantiated.

Apparently, these rumors are only kept alive in the interest of the pharmaceutical industry to scare people and to secure their prescription drug market. In the figure below, Dr. Rath's Vitamin Program is compared with therapies currently offered by conventional medicine. The potential side effects of these conventional drugs are listed with their references.

Conventional Medicine

Therapy	Potential Side Effects	References
Cholesterol-Lowering Drugs	Cancer, Liver Damage Myopathy (Muscle Weakness)	Physician's Desk Reference (PDR)
Aspirin	Strokes, Ulcers, Collagen Breakdown May Actually *Promote* Heart Disease	PDR Brooks
Calcium-Blocker	Cancer	Psaty

Cellular Medicine

Therapy	Potential Side Effects	References
Essential Nutrients	None	Bendich, This Book

207

How You Can Live Longer and Stay Healthy

Your body is as old as its cardiovascular system

The same biological mechanisms that lead to the hardening of arteries and to cardiovascular disease determine the process of aging in your body. One could say that aging of your body is a slow form of cardiovascular disease. The speed at which it ages is directly dependent from the state of health of your cardiovascular system. Particularly important is the optimum functioning of the 60,000-mile-long walls of your arteries, veins, and capillaries. This blood vessel pipeline supplies all organs of your body and billions of body cells with oxygen and essential nutrients.

If you do not protect your body with essential nutrients, the aging process leads to a gradual thickening of your blood vessel walls. This eventually leads to malnutrition of billions of your body cells, and to an accelerated aging of your entire body and its organs.

Dr. Rath's Vitamin Program is a proven way to protect your cardiovascular system. It is also the best way to help retard the aging process of your body in a natural way, thereby contributing to a long and healthy life.

Questions and Answers About Dr. Rath's Vitamin Program

Following are some of the questions most frequently asked about Dr. Rath's Vitamin Program. The responses are general recommendations and cannot replace a personal consultation with your doctor.

What is Dr. Rath's Vitamin Program?

It is a daily nutrient program composed of vitamins, amino acids, minerals and trace elements scientifically developed to optimize the function of the cardiovascular system. It is a program because the ingredients were chosen to work synergistically together. Ideally, it is complemented by moderate lifestyle changes as outlined in the 10-Step Program for Optimum Cardiovascular Health in the first chapter of this book.

Where can I get Dr. Rath's Vitamin Program?

Speak with the person who gave you this book. If you bought this book at the book store you can contact Dr. Rath's office directly through the numbers provided at the end of this book.

How can I make sure to get the original Cellular Medicine Vitamin Program?

Dr. Rath founded Cellular Medicine as the avenue to optimum health - independent of the pharmaceutical industry. Thus, the only reliable source for these formulas is the inventor of this new field of human health. At the end of this book you will find further information and adresses. Other companies may try to copy Cellular Medicine Programs which do not meet the high standards of Dr. Rath's research and development firm. Make sure that you get the original Cellular Medicine Formulas™.

What sets Dr. Rath's Vitamin Program apart from other multi-vitamins?

Dr. Rath's Vitamin Program is the first and only nutritional supplement program that is clinically tested and proven to halt

209

coronary heart disease already during its early stages. The message of this natural program helping to reverse even the most serious cardiovascular conditions including atherosclerosis, high blood pressure, heart failure and diabetic complications is spreading like a bush fire. Not surprisingly, within only a few years, Dr. Rath's Vitamin Program became the world's leading cardiovascular health program followed by tens of thousands of people in four continents.

Who can benefit from Dr. Rath's Vitamin Program?

Every man and woman, from teenager to seniors benefits from this program. Dr. Rath's *basic* Vitamin Program is primarily a preventive health program, helping to avoid cardiovascular problems in the first place. The amounts of the essential nutrients in this program may be increased in patients with cardiovascular disease, people under long-term physical or emotional stress, people living in cities with high air pollution, and elderly people.

How should Dr. Rath's Vitamin Program be taken?

Everyone should take 1 to 3 tablets daily of the *basic* Vitamin Program of Dr. Rath preferably with meals. Patients with existing health problems can take up to 12 tablets a day. In addition, complementary vitamin programs have been developed for specific health problems. These formulas should be taken *in conjuction with* the basic program. These complementary formulas are described at the end of each chapter throughout this book.

Are there any side effects of Dr. Rath's Vitamin Program?

All components of Dr. Rath's Vitamin Program are natural products. Therefore, your body is able to decide how much it needs of each of these ingredients. Side effects, such as those from overdosing of pharmaceutical drugs, do not occur even if you double or triple the dosages recommended in this book.

Is Dr. Rath's Vitamin Program a prescription item?
No. Dr. Rath's Vitamin Program is a nutritional supplement program, not a drug. It is available in any store where vitamins are sold.

Should I continue my regular prescription medication when starting on Dr. Rath's Vitamin Program?
Yes. If you are a patient, do not change or discontinue any prescription medication without consulting with your doctor. Dr. Rath's Vitamin Program is an adjunct to conventional therapy, not a substitute for your doctor's advice. You should also know that a growing number of doctors are already recommending Dr. Rath's Vitamin Program because it is scientifically based and clinically tested.

Is a healthy lifestyle more important than taking vitamins?
There is a misconception that needs to be clarified. The bioenergy components of Dr. Rath's Vitamin Program are the basis for any successful prevention and treatment of cardiovascular conditions. As explained in detail throughout this book, cardiovascular diseases develop because the cardiovascular cells are depleted of vitamins and other bioenergy fuel. Refilling this bioenergy is, therefore, the basic preventive and therapeutic measure for cardiovascular health. Life-style changes can add to these biological measures, but they are not able to replace them.

What about natural cardiovascular programs that build on heavy exercise, yoga or oriental philosophies?
Any cardiovascular health recommendation that does not include refilling of vitamins and other cellular bioenergy creates false hopes. These programs are outright dangerous. No heart patient has to become a fakir, triathlete or yoga master to optimize cardiovascular health. Moreover, a strict diet further aggravates the deficiencies of essential nutrients. For example, the artery "Teflon" amino acids lysine and proline are primarily contained in meat products. Don't be confused by self-appointed diet apostles and yoga masters. Vitamins and other

211

sources of cellular bioenergy remain the basis of natural cardiovascular health.

When can a patient expect health improvements with this vitamin program?

Every human being is different and the time it takes before health improvements are noticeable cannot be generalized. Patients with elevated blood pressure, irregular heart beat or shortness of breath, for example, may experience health improvements in the relatively short time of a few weeks. In contrast, the healing process for the artery walls and the reversal of atherosclerosis is a long-term process that requires months or years. Once your health has improved, you should be sure to continue using Dr. Rath's Vitamin Program in order to minimize the risk for recurrence of any health problems.

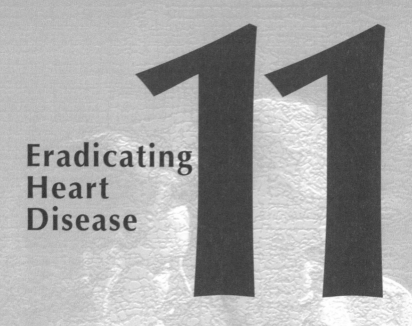

Eradicating
Heart
Disease

11

Why You May Not Have Heard About This Medical Breakthrough Before

When you read about the remarkable health benefits of vitamins throughout this book, you may have asked yourself, "Why is this life-saving information not used by every doctor and in every hospital? Why is the information that animals don't get heart attacks because they produce their own vitamin C not news on every TV and radio channel and on the front pages of newspapers?"

The answer is sobering: There is an entire industry with an innate economic interest to obstruct, suppress and discredit any information about the eradication of diseases. The pharmaceutical industry makes over one trillion dollars from selling drugs for ongoing diseases. These drugs may relieve symptoms, but they do not cure. We have to realize that the mission of this industry is to make money from *ongoing* diseases. The cure or eradication of a disease leads to the collapse of a multi-billion dollar market of pharmaceuticals.

I encourage you to read the following key points about the nature of the pharmaceutical business and to think about each of them. Now you will understand why we are bombarded with advertising campaigns by pharmaceutical companies wanting to make us believe that they are "Searching for Cures" "Striving for the Eradica-tion of Diseases" or "Increasing Life Expectancy" and other false promises. With these deceptive statements, the pharmaceutical industry has for decades been able to disguise the true nature of its business – maximum profit from ongoing diseases.

The Nature of the Pharmaceutical Industry

1. The natural purpose and driving force of the pharmaceutical industry is to increase sales of pharmaceutical drugs for ongoing diseases and to find new diseases to market existing drugs.

2. By this very nature, the pharmaceutical industry has no interest in curing diseases. The eradication of any disease inevitably destroys a multi-billion dollar market of prescription drugs as a source of revenues. Therefore, pharmaceutical drugs are primarily developed to relieve symptoms, but not to cure.

3. If eradication therapies for diseases are discovered and developed, the pharmaceutical industry has an inherent interest to suppress, discredit and obstruct these medical breakthroughs in order to make sure that diseases continue as the very basis for a lucrative prescription drug market.

4. The economic interest of the pharmaceutical industry itself is the main reason why no medical breakthrough has been made for the control of the most common diseases such as cardiovascular disease, high blood pressure, heart failure, diabetes, cancer, and osteoporosis, and why these diseases continue like epidemics on a worldwide scale.

6. For the same economic reasons, the pharmaceutical industry has now formed an international cartel by the code name "Codex Alimentarius" with the aim to outlaw any health information in connection with vitamins and to limit free access to natural therapies on a worldwide scale.

7. At the same time, the pharmaceutical companies withhold public information about the effects and risks of prescription drugs and life-threatening side effects are omitted or openly denied.

8. In order to assure the status quo of this deceptive scheme, a legion of pharmaceutical lobbyists is employed to influence legislation, control regulatory agencies (e.g. FDA), and manipulate medical research and education. Expensive advertising campaigns and PR agencies are used to deceive the public.

9. Millions of people and patients around the world are defrauded twice: A major portion of their income is used up to finance the exploding profits of the pharmaceutical industry. In return, they are offered a medicine that does not even cure.

More Deaths Than in All Wars of Mankind Combined

As a direct consequence of the pharmaceutical business, more people have died from preventable disease than in all wars of mankind combined. The following page summarizes the steps leading to this tragedy.

The fact that vitamin C stabilizes the walls of arteries, for example, has been known for 200 years, ever since James Lind uncovered vitamin C deficiency as the cause of blood loss and scurvy. Any head of a pharmaceutical company, any Ph.D. or M.D. who denies knowing this fact is simply incredulous. Why, then, was this information not applied to medicine in order to combat cardiovascular disease? Why was the official RDA for vitamin C set at 60 mg, an amount barely sufficient to prevent scurvy but certainly low enough to make sure that cardiovascular diseases will become an epidemic? The following page gives the answer.

Throughout this century, the pharmaceutical companies knew that an optimum vitamin supply of the population would lead to the collapse of a multi-billion dollar market of prescription drugs. Moreover, vitamins are not patentable and the profit margins are low. On the basis of this analysis the survival of the pharmaceutical industry became dependent on two strategies:
- To obstruct research, information, and use of vitamins and other natural therapies by all means available.
- To promote the deception that patentable synthetic drugs are the answer to human diseases.

The Pharmaceutical Industry Is Built on Two Deadly Columns

The Pharmaceutical Industry Is As Indispensable for a Country as Cancer Is for the Body

How is it that millions of people are still willing to pay billions of dollars to the pharma-cartel for medicine that does not cure and frequently harms?

The answer to this question is that over the past century the pharma-cartel and their army of lobbyists have built an intricate maze of control, infiltration, economic incentives, bribes, manipulation, and deception. The most important elements of this maze are summarized on the following page. Millions of people and patients were systematically deceived by this maze of

- **Manipulation** of research so that synthetic drugs rather than natural therapies appear as "medicine",

- **Prescription** of this "medicine" by doctors who have had no education in nutritional medicine and who receive financial benefits for prescribing pharmaceuticals but not natural therapies,

- **Deception** by multi-million dollar advertising campaigns for pharmaceutical drugs that deliberately deceive the public about the effects and risks of drugs and about the unethical nature of the pharma-business,

- **Regulation** brought about by regulatory agencies and legislation under the pressure of a pharma-lobby, disallowing established health claims for vitamins and other natural remedies.

In the future no nation can afford to burden its economy with a pharmaceutical industry that grows like a cancer at the expense of the people, of corporations and of the public sector, all of which suffocate from exploding health care costs for a medicine that does not cure.

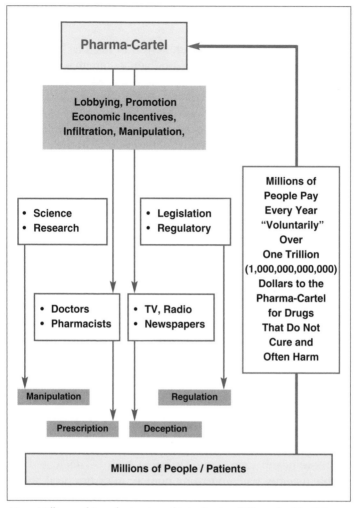

How Millions of People Are Lured into Paying Billions for Medicine That Does Not Cure

A New Era of Human Health Begins

500 years ago, the Roman church was making billions of Thaler (early dollars) by selling indulgences, an imaginary "key to heaven"for its believers. Then the fraud scheme collapsed and with it much of the power of the church. Today, the pharma business uses the same fraud scheme. It tries to sell the "key to health" to millions of people and takes away billions of dollars in return for an illusion: the deception that the pharmaceutical industry is interested in your health.

Considering this unhealthy state of affairs, the urgency for a new health care is obvious. The liberation from this insane yoke of the pharmaceutical industry will immediately and directly benefit millions of people, the business community and the public sector of all nations. This new health care system is based on an improved knowledge and participation by millions of people. Basic health has become understandable, doable and affordable for everyone. The era in human history when health was delegated to an industry that shamelessly took advantage of it is over and gone.

The new health care system focuses on primary health care, prevention and eradication of diseases. Health consultants and health centers will replace many medical high-tech centers of today. *Every health food store is the beginning for a community health center.*

The new health care system is being built by dedicated lay people together with a growing number of doctors and health professionals. The majority of health professionals are realizing that they themselves had been compromised by pharmaceutical companies and had become victims of a drug-centered health care.

Principles of a New Health Care System

1 **Health is understandable for everyone.** The basic causes of human health and disease are understandable for *everyone*. The fact that millions of body cells regularly need vitamins and other bioenergy supply can be understood by every child.

2 **Health is doable for everyone.** Cellular Medicine and the daily supply of vitamins and other bioenergy carriers allow *everyone* to maintain and to restore basic physical health.

3 **Health is safe for everyone.** Nature itself provides us with vitamins and other powerful preventive and therapeutic substances to combat human diseases. They are safe for everyone and without side effects.

4 **Health is affordable for everyone.** Effective health measures to prevent the most common human diseases can be offered in any country of the world at a fraction of today's cost. Imple-mentation of Cellular Medicine as a health measure immediately liberates trillions of dollars in private and public funds.

5 **Health is a human right.** Having access to optimum health is a basic human right. No pharmaceutical company and no government has the right to limit the spread of information about the health benefits of vitamins and other natural therapies. Every country in the world should amend its constitution to guarantee access to optimum health to its citizens.

6 **Effective health care focuses on prevention.** Future medical research and health care will focus on the prevention and eradication of diseases rather than on therapies that merely relieve the symptoms of diseases.

7 **Effective health care focuses on primary health care.** Community based primary health care is the key to an effective and affordable health care in any country of the world. Health consultants and health centers in every community will replace an ineffective and expensive focus on high-tech medicine.

8 **Medical research has to be under public control.** Public funds for medical research should primarily be used to develop treatments that *prevent* and *eradicate* diseases, rather than on merely relieving symptoms and creating dependencies.

The Process of Eradicating Heart Disease Has Become Irreversible

The following chapter highlights the historic development behind this book. It is based on a presentation by Dr. Rath at a recent Conference of the *American Academy for the Advancement in Medicine* and has been updated for this book.

Only rarely comes the privilege of being present at the moment of triumph in the control of a major disease, and, for cardiovascular disease, that moment is now. Over half a century ago the Canadian cardiologist, J.C. Paterson, published the first clinical studies that vitamin deficiency is a primary cause for heart attacks and strokes. Each year, more than 12 million people die worldwide from heart attacks and strokes. Since Dr. Paterson's studies, over half a billion people have died from cardiovascular disease, more than in all wars of mankind together. Throughout this century, cardiovascular disease has become one of the largest epidemics in the history of mankind. Now, at the end of this century, we have to realize that most of these deaths could have been prevented and that the cardiovascular epidemic could have been controlled long ago by an optimum intake of vitamins and other essential nutrients.

I am often asked: "If this knowledge had been used in medicine, could my father, sister, uncle or son still be alive?" The answer is "Yes, very likely!" Why did so many people have to die? The main reason is the non-patentability of vitamins and the massive economic interest of pharmaceutical companies. Pioneering scientists and health professionals deserve credit for their advocacy of vitamins and other natural therapies. Among them are Irwin Stone, Linus Pauling, Abram Hoffer and many others. Despite their noble efforts and until very recently the opposing pharmaceutical interest groups prevailed and continued to control public opinion by discrediting the health benefits of vitamins. As a consequence, hundreds of thousands of

physicians and other health professionals and millions of people around the world were deceived and remained misin-
formed and biased against the health benefits of vitamins.

Now, on tthe turn of this century, everything is changing. Vitamins suddenly make the front pages of newspapers and they
are on national TV news almost every week. The American
Medical Association suddenly endorses the use of vitamins in
the fight against heart disease, and legislation allowing health
claims for vitamins is being discussed. The groundwork for this
change of perception in favor of vitamins has been laid over
many decades. However, the trigger for the current large-scale
acceptance of vitamins came from the field of science, from a
medical advance, which will lead to the control of cardiovascular diseases during the next few decades.

Here I would like to share with you an account of this advance
in cardiovascular health, of the milestones we have already
passed, the obstacles we have overcome and of the breathtak-
ing perspective towards an improvement of human health on a
global level.

The background

In 1990, I came to America with a discovery in my suitcase
that would lead to a new scientific rationale of cardiovascular
diseases. The message was clear: Vitamins are the key to the
control of cardiovascular disease, the number one killer in the
industrialized world. But this breakthrough was not immediately embraced. When I decided to give up my clinical career
to pursue this research avenue, many of my colleagues in Germany warned me that working on vitamins would ruin my
career.

During 1989 I presented lectures and introduced my research
project to leading cardiovascular research centers in America -
among them Baylor College of Medicine in Houston, University of Chicago, National Institutes of Health, and the Univer-

*The cooperation and friendship with two-time Nobel Laureate
Linus Pauling was so close, that Pauling asked Dr. Rath to continue
his life work. In the centre of the picture Dr. Pauling's secretary
Dorothy Munro*

sity of California at La Jolla. Everywhere the new risk factor, lipoprotein(a), was met with great interest - but working on vitamins was still considered too controversial. In early 1990 I accepted the invitation of Linus Pauling to work with him, only to discover that at age 89 he had become tired of fighting and a breakthrough for vitamins in medicine was nowhere in sight. Heartened by my discoveries, he and I founded two companies in order to jump-start this process.

1990 was also the year when America's worst prescription drug disaster came to light. An estimated 50,000 Americans died from taking an antiarrhythmic drug that actually caused arrest of the heart beat and sudden cardiac death. This was the same number of people killed in the Vietnam War. A Congressional investigation established that the FDA had approved this drug without any controlled clinical studies. This tragedy is presented in Thomas Moore's book *Deadly Medicine*, a "must-read" for everyone. Thus, while drug research had reached another deadlock, vitamins and essential nutrients as effective and safe alternatives were still ostracized by conventional medicine and restricted by the regulatory climate.

Nutritional medicine was a stepchild in America, but the situation was even worse in Europe. When you wanted to ship a bottle of 1,000 milligram tablets of Vitamin C to Germany, it was returned by customs because vitamin C pills above 500 milligrams are considered drugs. This was the state of affairs only five years ago. It is with this background that we can truly appreciate the milestones we have reached and the obstacles we were able to remove in the meantime. In the next part of my talk I would like to give you an account of this process from my personal experience.

Milestone 1:
Breakthrough Discovery
The first step towards control of cardiovascular disease was discovery of the connection between lipoprotein (a) and vitamin C. The human body produces the risk factor, lipoprotein (a) to compensate for loss of the body's own vitamin C production. As a result, every second human being dies from heart attacks

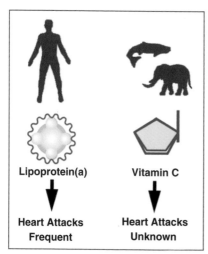

*The Lipoprotein(a)-
Vitamin C Connection*

Lipoprotein(a)   **Vitamin C**

Heart Attacks   **Heart Attacks**
Frequent   **Unknown**

225

and strokes, while cardiovascular diseases are essentially unknown in the animal world. This discovery attracted my interest in vitamin research.

By 1991 the conceptual work was completed and I summarized it in two scientific articles: *Solution to the Puzzle of Human Cardiovascular Disease* and *A Unified Theory of Human Cardiovascular Disease Leading the Way to the Abolition of This Diseases as a Cause of Human Mortality*. These publications presented for the first time the scientific rationale that heart attacks and strokes are preventable and that cardiovascular disease can be eradicated. I invited as co-author Linus Pauling, who agreed to support these far-reaching conclusions.

Milestone 2:
Entirely new Understanding of the Nature of
Cardiovascular Disease
The new understanding about the nature of cardiovascular disease is presented in detail in the first chapters of this book. This new understanding clarified that the primary cause of cardiovascular disease is not high cholesterol or a fatty diet. These factors can only become risk factors if the wall of our arteries is already weakened by vitamin deficiency - and only then.

It became also clear that atherosclerotic plaques in our arteries are not preordained events; these plaques are nothing but a scaffold of Nature trying to stabilize and repair the blood vessel walls during vitamin deficiency. Finally, this new scientific rationale can also explain why we get infarctions of the heart and not the nose or ears.

Obviously, a new scientific rationale that could suddenly explain so many unsolved mysteries about the number one health problem would not go unnoticed. At that time, it became clear to the pharmaceutical companies and to the medical opinion leaders that the cholesterol dogma and a huge prescription drug market would eventually collapse. The time this would take was only dependent on one factor: How fast can the discovery of the scurvy-heart disease connection be spread globally. Thus it was in 1990 that a giant battle for public perceptions started, with a multi-billion dollar industry fighting for its survival.

But there were also other voices early on. One of the first congratulations came from the head of Cardiology of Harvard Medical School, Professor Valentin Fuster. In July 1992 he wrote me, "You may be quite correct in your predictions about the role of vitamin C in cardiovascular disease", and he announced that his own department would start in this line of research.

Milestone 3:
Media Support for Vitamins
The next step in this process was the key media support for vitamins and nutritional medicine. The title story, *The Real Power of Vitamins* in the April 1992 issue of *TIME Magazine* was triggered by an international conference on vitamins held by the New York Academy of Sciences in February of that year. Many scientists contributed to this conference. I was privileged to be one of them and to introduce our new understanding about the nature of cardiovascular disease, including the key role of vitamins and its prevention.

After decades of bias and boycott against vitamins in the media, this issue of *TIME* Magazine became a watershed event, and media coverage about vitamins changed forever. From then on, essentially every epidemiological study showing the benefits of vitamins in the prevention of cardiovascular disease made front page news. Only weeks after this *TIME* Magazine article, an important epidemiological study by

227

James Enstrom and his colleagues from the University of Los Angeles, received national attention. It showed that long-term vitamin C supplementation, as opposed to the average American diet, could cut the rate for heart disease almost in half. Thus the suddenly available and positive media coverage led to a change of perception in favor of vitamins, with worldwide repercussions.

Milestone 4:
Empowerment of the Patients
Because this new understanding about the Nature of cardiovascular disease had direct and immediate importance for the health and the lives of millions of people, it had to be presented in a language understandable to everyone. My popular science book *Eradicating Heart Disease* and *Why Animals Don't Get Heart Attacks*, precisely serve this purpose.

Why was this step so important? A hundred years ago, when bacteria were discovered as the cause of infectious diseases, it still took several decades before the first antibiotics and vaccines were developed. Now, with the breakthrough in cardiovascular disease, no such time is needed. Vitamins and other essential nutrients, the solution to the cardiovascular epidemic, are available for everyone right now. Thus, the time it takes to control the cardiovascular epidemic depends on one main factor – the time it takes to spread the message about the health benefits of vitamins. These books were written to serve precisely this purpose and they have already empowered tens of thousands of people to take a greater responsibility for their own health. Patients now go back to their doctors, many of whom are still skeptical, and present this valuable information about the health benefits of vitamins to them.

This growing avalanche did not go unnoticed. During the last two years, major medical schools, the American Heart Association, and the pharmaceutical industry followed with their own versions of cardiovascular "self-help" books and information brochures. But their information lacked the decisive message: Vitamins and other essential nutrients are the solution to the cardiovascular epidemic.

Milestone 5:

The Natural reversal of Cardiovascular Disease is Officially Regognized

The next important step in this process was the granting by the US Patent Office of the world's first patents to reverse heart disease without surgery. This was the first time that a patent had been issued for a natural process to *reverse* atherosclerotic deposits and cardiovascular disease. The details of new therapeutic technology are described in the first chapters of my book.

Milestone 6:

New Legislation Guarantees Free Access to Vitamins

Thus, while the U.S. Patent Office, a Federal Agency, issued patents for the use of vitamins to reverse cardiovascular disease, the U.S. Food and Drug Administration (FDA), another Federal Agency, tried to make these essential nutrients prescription drugs. Why did the FDA start this battle in 1991 and why was it the fiercest FDA attack on nutritional supplements thus far? I have already given the answer: If vitamins are the solution to the cardiovascular epidemic – a prescription drug market of over 100 billion dollars annually is going to collapse.

The Nutritional Health and Education Act from1994 Guarantees Free Access to Vitamins

In August 1994 the U.S. Congress passed legislation preserving free access to vitamins and other essential nutrients.

229

This victory in the battle for vitamin freedom has a truly historic dimension and it provided an important window of opportunity that can now be used to win similar battles in other countries. Many contributed to this historic success, but most important were those millions of Americans who made it unmistakably clear to their political representatives that they will have free access to their vitamins today – and in the future! My first book *Eradicating Heart Disease* contained an Open Letter to the US-President. As an Open Letter, the primary addressees were the American people, in order to empower them to take a stand on this important issue. Health food store owners informed me that copies of this "Open Letter to the President" were picked up in their stores by the hundreds, together with the petitions to political representatives to halt the plans of the FDA. Thus, the medical breakthrough in vitamin and heart disease research that triggered this battle also became a contributing factor to win it.

Milestone 7:
Cellular Medicine – Foundation of a New Health Care System
The next step was to lay the ground for a new health care system that is no longer dependent on the pharmaceutical industry. Cellular Medicine since has become synonymous for the worldwide change in medicine. Based on the breakthrough discoveries described in this book, we developed natural health programs which today are available around the world. At the same time this medical breakthrough was featured on the internet. Today the website www.drrath.com has become the leading resource location on the internet for natural health information.

Milestone 8:
The Flood Gates of Established Medicine are Opening
By 1995 the news of the current book "Why Animals Don't Get Heart Attacks - But People Do" was spreading like a wildfire and reached the doctor's offices across America. In the following months the flood gates of established medicine against

The Worst Defeat of the FDA in its History

At the beginning of this decade, almost all "experts" of the FDA were on the payroll of pharmaceutical companies and the FDA had turned into a puppet arm of the pharmaceutical industry. Hidden behind this Federal Agency, the Pharma-Cartel attacked. It was clear that hundreds of millions of Americans who had been enjoying free access to vitamins over decades would not understand why the FDA suddenly wants to make vitamins prescription drugs. Thus, a PR camouflage had to be presented to the public to make these unethical plans palatable and acceptable:

- **"Consumer Protection"** In a large-scale public relations campaign the FDA, on behalf of the Pharma-Cartel, tried to make millions of Americans believe that vitamins and other natural therapies had to become prescription items in order to protect them from "overdosing." The house of cards collapsed when the following U.S. statistics became public: From 1983 to 1990, not a single death resulted from intake of vitamins, amino acids, or other natural products. In contrast, during the same period, almost one million Americans died as a consequence of taking prescription drugs which had been approved by the FDA!

- **"Internationalization"** The second cover name under which the FDA and the Cartel tried to limit free access to vitamins was the alleged necessity for internationally unified guidelines for vitamins. Perhaps with their eyes on Germany and other European countries, where one gram vitamin C pills are defined as prescription drugs and where amino acids are on the "black list", these special interest groups tried to turn nutritional medicine back to medieval times.

But the American people were neither interested in "consumer protection" from vitamins nor in "internationalization" back to the medieval ages. In the "largest movement since the Vietnam War" *(Newsweek)* the American People through their political representatives, secured Vitamin Freedom and defeated the FDA and the Pharma-Cartel.

231

vitamins broke and essential nutrients entered conventional medicine on a broad front.

- On June 21, the *Journal of the American Medical Association* (JAMA), published for the first time an article on the use of antioxidant vitamins as a basic treatment for coronary heart disease.

- In October, 1995, the leading medical schools in America decided to establish departments of nutritional medicine in order to provide to future generations of doctors with a basic understanding about the health benefits of vitamins and other essential nutrients.

- In November, 1995, the National Institutes of Health (NIH) decided to give multi-million dollar research grants to ten leading research institutions in America, among them Stanford University, to study "alternative" treatments, including vitamin therapy.

- The leading medical schools, including Harvard University, started to recommend vitamins as basic health measures in patient brochures, self-help books, and community newsletters.

These developments are no coincidence; they are brought about by the message of this book. They are long overdue and they will change medicine forever.

Milestone 9:
First Victory Against the Pharma-Cartel at the International Level
With the battle to make vitamins prescription items in the U.S. lost, the pharmaceutical industry decided to regroup at the international level. Now they decided to start a campaign to outlaw worldwide all preventive and therapeutic health information about vitamins and other natural therapies. Towards this end the pharma industry founded the *international*

Pharma-Cartel with the main goal to abuse the United Nations in order to ban any natural health claims in all UN member countries. The Pharma-Cartel's thrust is being led through the World Health Organization's "Codex Alimentarius" Commission, wherein the decisive Committee is headed by the German Pharma-Cartel. Moreover, the name "Codex Alimentarius" was an ideal cover to camouflaged the efforts of the Cartel as "consumer protection".

The "Codex"-Cartel is a desperate effort of the international pharmaceutical industry to secure its survival as we know it today. If they lose this international battle, similar to the defeat in the U.S., vitamins will become accepted worldwide as powerful preventive and therapeutic agents, benefitting millions of people – and substantially reducing the markets for pharmaceutical pills.

Particularly noteworthy has been the political support for the unethical "Codex" plans by the previous German government. The background: German Ex-Chancellor Helmut Kohl's first employer was the German Pharma-Cartel. From 1959 to 1969 he worked as a lobbyist for the Verband der Chemischen Industrie (VCI), the lobby centrale of the German Pharma-Cartel. Evidently, this interest group was able to promote one of their own lobbyists into the highest office of government. For 16 years an ex-pharma lobbyist governed the world's third largest industrial nation on behalf of the Pharma-Cartel and used his political position to influence world affairs on behalf of his former employers. The close connection between the pharmaceutical industry and government in Germany throughout the 20th century is summarized on the previous page.

Until September 1998 the German government was the political spearhead of the international Pharma-Cartel and of its efforts to ban of all therapeutic health information in connection with vitamins and other natural therapies. To make sure these controversial laws would go through in countries where resistance would be strong, such as the U.S., the Cartel has

233

The Fateful Alliance Between the Pharmaceutical Cartel and the German Government Throughout the 20th Century

Germany is often described as the "pharmacy of the world" and large US companies, such as Merck, have their origin in this country. The largest pharmaceutical multinationals based in Germany, BASF, Bayer, and Hoechst have subsidiaries in over 120 countries. Throughout this century these multinationals have had a devastating influence on world affairs.

- In the 1920s BASF, Bayer and Hoechst formed the first Cartel, IG Farben.

- In 1932 IG Farben gave 400,000 German Marks to finance Hitler's election campaign, the single largest donation of any company. The Nuremberg Tribunal stated: Without the IG Farben World War II would not have been possible.

- In return, IG Farben participated in the plunder of all countries conquered by the NAZI Wehrmacht, including Austria, Czechoslovakia, Poland, Norway, Holland, Belgium, France and the rest of Europe.

Scene from Steven Spielberg's film "Schindler's List". The Auschwitz concentration camp was a forced labor outpost of the IG Auschwitz, a 100% subsidiary of IG Farben.

- In 1941, IG Farben established the world's largest chemical factory in Auschwitz, taking advantage of cheap labor from the Auschwitz concentration camp. The Zyklon-B gas, used to exterminate millions of victims in the gas chambers, came from the IG Farben laboratories.

- At the Nuremberg War Tribunal 24 IG Farben executives were convicted of mass murder, slavery, plundering and other crimes, but by 1951 all of them were back in business.

- The Nuremberg War Tribunal dissected the IG Farben into BASF, Bayer and Hoechst, but the tradition continued: Until the 1970s the board chairmen of all three companies were former members of the NAZI Party: Carl Wurster (BASF), Curt Hansen (Bayer) and Carl Winnacker (Hoechst).

- The Cartel tradition of the IG Farben continued under a new name, the *Verband der Chemischen Industrie, VCI* (Association of Chemical Industry).

- Even the tradition of raising servile politicians continued. German *Ex*-Chancellor Helmut Kohl was a 10 year lobbyist for the very same VCI, before he became a politician. With the financial and PR support of the Cartel he became Chancellor of Germany and served the global interests of the Pharma-Cartel.

Helmut Kohl (center) and his chief advisors and his Cartel bosses: Juergen Dormann (Hoechst, left) and Juergen Strube (BASF, right).

235

threatened international trade sanctions in case of non-compliance. If the people and the governments of the United Kingdom, the United States, Canada, Australia or any other country refuse to accept vitamins as prescription drugs, the Pharma-Cartel, would impose UN trade sanctions for other industries from that country. With this strategy the Pharma-Cartel has tried to force the entire corporate world at its side and, at the same time, has declared war on the health interests of millions of people.

By the end of 1996 the Pharma-Cartel's "Codex"-Plans had already reached stage 5 of an 8-stage process within the United Nations, Covered as "consumer protection" these unconscionable plans were about to be recommended to the UN General Assembly for adoption. This was the situation until June 21, 1997. On that day Dr. Rath gave a speech for 3,400 people in Chemnitz, Germany. He revealed the connection between the "Codex" Cartel, the German Government and its roots in the tradition of those companies responsible for World War II and the holocaust. With a view on the devastating consequences of the "Codex" plans for global human health he stated:

"Twice in this century, indescribable worldwide suffering and death originated from Germany. This must not happen a third time."

This speech was immediately distributed via the Internet. In addition, audio tapes and video tapes of this historic spech became available. Today hundreds of thousands of them are circulating. Together with the spread of Dr. Rath's book in Germany, the "Chemnitz Programm" became a political topic in the living rooms and in the streets of Germany.

Black September for the Pharmaceutical Cartel

The next severe set-back for the pharmaceutical cartel's Codex plans came in September 1998, which can justifiably be described as the "Black September for the Pharmaceutical Cartel". On 27 September 1998, pharmaceutical lobbyist and Federal Chancellor Kohl was swept out of office after 16 years as a result of an overwhelming vote of no confidence from the people.

Busting the Vitamin Cartel

On May 20, 1999, the media bomb detonated: The pharmaceutical multinational corporation Hoffmann-La Roche, BASF, Rhône-Poulenc and other multinational pharmaceutical companies admitted to have formed a so-called "Vitamin-Cartel" to conduct criminal price fixing for vitamin raw materials. Hundreds of millions of people worldwide were defrauded for almost a decade and had to pay higher vitamin prices because of this criminal activities. The US-justice departement declared that this Vitamin-Cartel was the largest cartel ever discovered and named it an economic "conspiracy". Roche, BASF and the others cartel members agreed to pay almost a billion dollars in fines for committing these crimes.

While the magnitude of these fines made headlines around the world, the events that triggered the formation of this criminal cartel remained obscure. Until now. The background of this illegal Vitamin-Cartel is the scientific breakthrough documented in this book in relation to vitamins and prevention of cardiovascular disease. Already in the beginning of 1990 I informed the Swiss multinational pharmaceutical company Hoffmann-La Roche about these discoveries. On June 2, 1990, I send the summary of the discovery that heart attacks and strokes are – similar to scurvy – the result of vitamin C deficiency to Prof. Jürgen Drews, head of Roche research worldwide and member of its executive board.

Roche is the world's leading manufacturer of vitamin C raw material. The Roche executives realized immediately that my discovery will boost their international demand for vitamin C and create a multi-billion dollar market for vitamin C and other viatmins. In order to get further information from me, the executives of Hoffmann-La Roche signed a confidentiality agreement and invited me to represent the new understanding of heart disease at their global headquarter in Basel, Switzerland. However, Roche decided *not* to promote this medical breakthrough, despite the fact that they acknowledged it as a breakthrough. The reasons they gave to me in writing: Roche did not want to finance the dissemination of this understanding of heart disease for all their competitors and they did not want to compete with other in-house pharmaceutical drug developments, such as cholesterol-lowering drugs.

Thus, while they refused to promote this medical breakthrough that could have saved millions of lives, this pharmaceutical companies turned around and decided to conspire in form of a vitamin Cartel in order to take advantage of this medical breakthrough anyway. Roche apparently invited BASF, Rhone-Poulenc, Takeda and other manufacturers of vitamin raw materials to criminal price fixing on a global level. The fraudulent profits these companies made from their criminal practices are estimated over 100 billion dollars over the past ten years. Compared to that, the fines these companies had to pay are nothing less than peanuts.

Not only the US government should receive compensation for the damage these companies have done, but vitamin companies and above all consumers world-wide should sue these companies in class action law suites all over the world. This is even more urgent, since these companies have harmed millions of people twice: First, they refused to promote and disseminate the live-saving information on the use of vitamins in order to prevent heart disease, thereby causing millions of heart patients to die unnecessarily over the past ten years. Second, they caused financial damage to literally every vitamin consumer on earth.

My correspondence with the Roche executives also proves the statements by Hoffmann-La Roche as a lie that the leadership

238

June 4, 1990

Professor Jürgen Drews
Hoffmann-La Roche & Co. AG
Grenzacherstrasse 122
Basel
CH-4058 Baselstadt
Switzerland

Dear Professor Drews:

Following our conversation on the vitamin C-related atherosclerosis research we send you today the concept of this work. ... ... The implications of this concept for human health are obvious. Our research promises to provide important missing links on the cellular and molecular level to prove the role of vitamin C on prevention and therapy for cardiovascular disease and other diseases. Beside animal studies conducted, we have obtained preliminary data from patients in support of this concept. If further evidence can be provided, we foresee a several-fold increase in the preventive and therapeutic use of vitamin C.

As a next step we suggest that further evidence should be provided on various research levels. We could offer links to other research labs and clinical centers interested in this field.

We are convinced of the mutual benefit of our discovery and its scientific and commercial impacts. We are looking forward to your reply.

Sincerely,

Dr. Matthias Rath

MR:mb

‹Roche›

F. HOFFMANN-LA ROCHE AG

Law Department

Your Ref.: MR:
Our Ref.: StA/Co-mb
Direct Dialling: 061 688 58 66   Basel, June 18, 1990

Agreement of Confidentiality

Dear Dr. Rath,

We are refering to the draft Agreement of Confidentiality of May 25, 1990, already signed by you.

May we kindly ask you to send us a second original of the Agreement of Confidentialty already duly signed by you. After full execution of both originals, we shall return to you one original and keep the other one for our files.

Yours sincerely,

F.HOFFMANN-LA ROCHE Ltd

Prof. J. Drews   Dr. C. Conti

CH-4002 Basel, Schweiz
Telephon 061-688 11 11
Telex 962 292/965 542 hlr ch
Telefax 061-691 93 91/691 96 00

F.HOFFMANN-LA ROCHE LTD
CH-4002 Basel, Switzerland
Telephone 061-688 11 11
Telex 962 292/965 542 hlr ch
Telefax 061-691 93 91/691 96 00

F.HOFFMANN-LA ROCHE SA
CH-4002 Bâle, Suisse
Téléphone 061-688 11 11
Télex 962 292/965 542 hlr ch
Téléfax 061-691 93 91/691 96 00

of Roche did not know about these criminal activities. The opposite is now clear: The executives of Roche, BASF, Rhône-Poulenc and others did not only know about these crimes, they were the organizers. The mangers responsible for these crimes up to the highest levels of these companies have to be prosecuted and held responsible for their actions. But already today everyone can call those companies and their leadership as criminals, who distinguish themselves from a street robber only by the magnitude of their crimes. The criminal activities of this vitamin Cartel have opened millions of people the eyes even further about the "business with disease" maintained by the pharmaceutical industry. The scandal of the vitamin Cartel has only just begun but it has already become another major nail in the coffin of the pharmaceutical industry.

The Berlin Tribunal

The most recent full assembly of the Codex Alimentarius Commission took place in June 2000 in Berlin. The aim of the meeting was a world-wide ban on health information concerning natural healing methods, in order to keep alive artificially a pharmaceutical market worth billions. To camouflage its activities, the pharmaceutical cartel and its political accomplices hid away from 19 - 23 June in the so-called "Federal Office for Consumer Health Protection" (BgVV), which was hermetically sealed behind barbed wire.

On the evenings before, 17 and 18 June, I held a conference against the pharmaceutical cartel in Berlin, as I had also done two years previously in September 1998. The "Berlin Tribunal", which in the meantime has become a historic document, can be read in full on our website. I publicly demanded that the pharmaceutical managers and their political accomplices should be indicted for "crimes against humanity".

On Monday 19 June, the first day of the Codex conference, my co-workers gave each of the official Codex delegates from more than 40 countries an English-language copy of the plans and intentions of the pharmaceutical cartel. As a result, the debate in the Codex Commission was so vigorous that the pharmaceutical cartel's plans could not gain acceptance at this full assembly either.

A breathtaking perspective

There is no doubt: The turn from the second into the third millennium coincides with a change in a health care world-wide. Millions of people are waking up and realizing that they had become dependent on a false health care system that was little more than an illusion. In daily raising numbers patients and health professionals alike are taking advantage of the fact that the most common diseases of our time can be effectively prevented and treated by vitamins and other essential nutrients. Many thousands of people worldwide are already working in our international health-consulting network with the goal to implement a new health care system. Most of our consultants are patients who have been deceived and defrauded over decades by a conventional medicine. With the help of vitamin research and our Cellular Medicine Formulas, these patients have regained a life that is worth living. Many thousands of these patients in Europe, America and all other continents are living proof that a new health care system has already become reality.

The health improvements achieved with our Cellular Medicine Formulas are so superior to conventional medical approaches for cardiovascular disease, cancer and other common diseases that the first large health insurance companies in Europe are reimbursing the costs for these formulas. The basis for this decision, of course, was that the health improvements with our Cellular Medicine Formulas were documented beyond any doubt.

I'm inviting you, the readers of this book, to make your own judgement about the efficacy of our Cellular Medicine Formulas. If you are convinced, I invite you to join our international network of health consultants and actively help to pass on this live saving information to others. Millions of lives are at stake. The time to act is now.

The Pharma-Cartel runs amok

Great Britain

Even after all these defeats, the Pharma-Cartel is not giving in. Now they try to cement their rule by twisting the arms of national governments and international parliamentary bodies such as the European Community. A particularly striking example of the desperation of the Pharma-Cartel is a new legislation that is currently being pushed through the British Parliament under the cover name MLX 249. This law foresees to criminalize the dissemination of any preventive or therapeutic health information in relation to vitamins and other natural health remedies. Even worse, the pharmaceutical industry demands the judicial power in order to judge and punish any violations under this proposed legislation.

The Netherlands

In the Netherlands the Pharma-Cartel organized a coup to bring down the Dutch government. One member of parliament, Senator Wiegel, the gatekeeper of the Pharma-Cartel in the Dutch health insurance industry, casted the decisive vote that almost brought down the government of prime minister Kok. In a second attempt, they attacked the pharma-critical Health Minister Els Borst in an attempt to force her to resign from office. Both crises were planned and carried out on behalf of the Pharma-Cartel. Fortunately, the people and politicians in the Netherlands found out about it and were smart enough to defeat these acts of political sabotage.

USA

In the USA the Pharma-Cartel is making a new attack on natural health information and products. Only weeks after the house bank of the German Pharma-Cartel, Deutsche Bank, took over the US bank Banker's Trust to become the largest bank in the world, their influence on the US-Government became visible. Five years after the pharmaceutical industry and the FDA had experienced their largest defeat in the USA ever, the German Pharma-Cartel directly organized their first attack on US soil. This time they did not use the FDA as their front organization rather than the Federal Trade Commission (FTC). Pushed by the international Pharma-Cartel, the US-FTC announced a nation-wide campaign with the sarcastic name "Operation Cure All". The goals and the hypocrisy of this effort can be reviewed in detail on our website. The goal of this witch hunt by the FTC is the same as it was 5 years ago with the FDA: Preventing the dissemination of live saving health information on vitamins and other natural and non-patentable products in order to protect and promote a multi-billion dollar market of unnecessary pharmaceutical drugs.

PETITION FOR VITAMIN FREEDOM

Each year the pharmaceutical companies make several hundred billions of dollars solely from world-wide sales of cardiovascular drugs. The natural control of the cardiovascular epidemic will lead to a collapse of this market and threatens the existence of this industry.

In their struggle for survival the pharmaceutical industry has formed a globally operating "Pharma-Cartel" aiming to block the world-wide spread of this life-saving information. By abusing the World Health Organization's "Codex Alimentarius" Commission, this Cartels seeks the following binding legislation for all member countries of the Unbited Nations:

1 a world-wide ban on all information about the preventive and therapeutic health benefits in connection with vitamins, minerals, amino acids and other essential nutrients,

2 outlawing free access to essential nutrients which exceed the arbitrarily low dosage recommendations of the "Codex",

3 imposing international trade sanctions upon nations not willing to implement these "recommendations" into national laws.

Despite growing worldwide resistance, the "Codex" Cartel continues. In this situation, millions of people world-wide have to protect their own health and lives against the interests of this pharmaceutical industry cartel. World-wide free access to vitamins will be the first victory on our way towards the eradication of heart disease.

We demand that our own government and the governments of all other countries:
- **abolish all barriers restricting free access to vitamins and other essential nutrients,**
- **spread the life-saving information about health benefits of vitamins and other natural therapies,**
- **Promote the eradication of heart disease by supporting vitamin research and by all other means available.**

With my signature I support the International Declaration "21st Century – the Century of Eradicating Heart Disease" and the Worldwide Petition for Vitamin Freedom:

Name	Address	Signature

I encourage you to support this important cause with your signature. Please make copies of these pages and ask your family, friends, neighbors, and colleagues for their signatures and support. Discuss this Declaration and Petition at your workplace, school, or church and introduce it to your health care provider, insurance company and to other organizations you are affiliated with; urge their support for these world-wide initiatives. Please send your signed support back to my personal attention: MR Publishing Inc., Postbus 859, 7600 AW Almelo, The Netherlands. We will count the signatures regularly and publish the total numbers as ongoing documentation of the growing worldwide support for this noble cause.

245

How You Can Contribute to Eradicating Heart Disease

How long it will take until people in your country will be able to make use of this medical breakthrough now also depends on you. What can you do?

- Pass this book on to relatives, neighbors, colleagues, friends and to your doctor.

- Contact your newspapers, radio and TV stations, in order to help spread this information through the media.

- Copy the Declaration, Petition and the signature list and urge all organizations you are affiliated with to familiarize themselves with its content.

- Write to the representatives in your city council and your regional and federal governments. Attach a short letter in support of these documents and add your own comments.

- Visit your political representatives personally and put this book on their table. Tell your representatives to stand up against the "Codex" Cartel and ask them what they will do to help spread the information about the life-saving health benefits of vitamins. Plan the visit to your political representatives with some friends who share this concern.

The new era of human health will be build on health information, education and health empowerment of the public at large. Patients and lay people will become natural health consultants and consulting centers for Cellular Medicine will be created. You are encouraged to become an architect of this new health care system.

Things You Can Do to Help:

1.

2.

3.

4.

5.

6.

7.

8.

Do it for yourself and for the generation of your children and grandchildren.

Notes

Appendix 12

The Rath-Pauling Manifesto

The following document was handwritten by Linus Pauling and signed by him in the names of two scientists, Dr. Pauling and Dr. Rath. With this last public appeal, Linus Pauling supported the scientific breakthrough reported in this book. With this historic document the two-time Nobel Laureate with his own hand passed on the torch of nutritional research to the next generation.

First and last page of this historic document in Linus Pauling's own hand writing.

Dr. Pauling and Dr. Rath at the Press Conference.

CALL FOR AN INTERNATIONAL EFFORT TO ABOLISH HEART DISEASE

Heart disease, stroke, and other forms of cardiovascular disease now kill millions of people every year and cause millions more to be disabled. There now exists the opportunity to reduce greatly this toll of death and disability by the optimum dietary supplementation with vitamins and other essential nutrients.

During recent years we and our associates have made two remarkable discoveries. One is that the primary cause of heart disease is the insufficient intake of ascorbate (vitamin C), an insufficiency from which nearly every person on earth suffers. Ascorbate deficiency leads to weakness of the walls of the arteries and to the initiation of the atherosclerotic process, particularly in stressed regions. We conclude that cholesterol and other blood risk factors increase the risk for heart disease only if the wall of the artery is weakened by ascorbate deficiency.

The other discovery is that the main cholesterol transporting particle forming atherosclerotic plaques is not LDL (low density lipoprotein) but a related lipoprotein, lipoprotein (a). Moreover, certain essential nutrients, especially the amino acid L-lysine, can block the deposition of this lipoprotein and may even reduce existing plaques. We have concluded that the optimum supplementation of ascorbate and some other nutrients could largely prevent heart disease and stroke and be effective in treating existing disease. Published clinical and epidemiological data support this conclusion.

The goal is now in sight: the abolition of heart disease as the cause of disability and mortality for the present generation and future generations of human beings.

WITH MILLIONS OF LIVES EACH YEAR AT STAKE NO TIME SHOULD BE LOST!

- We call upon our colleagues in science and medicine to join in a vigorous international effort, on the levels of both basic research and clinical studies, to investigate the value of vitamin C and other nutrients in controlling heart disease.
- We call upon the national and international health authorities and other health institutions to support this effort with political and financial measures.
- We call upon every human being to encourage local medical institutions and physicians to take an active part in this process.

THE GOAL OF ELIMINATING HEART DISEASE AS THE MAJOR CAUSE OF DEATH AND DISABILITY IS NOW IN SIGHT!

Matthias Rath and Linus Pauling

251

Continuing the Life Work of Linus Pauling

Whenever a major scientific breakthrough occurs, such as the eradication of cardiovascular disease, there exists a legitimate public interest in learning more about the background of the discovery. Who made the discovery, when and where? I decided that the best way to answer these questions is to share the documents on the opposite page with you. By signing these documents, Dr. Linus Pauling acknowledged the need to clarify the following issues for everyone to know and for posterity:

- who made these discoveries
- to whom they belong
- his will about the continuation of his life work.

I had personally known Linus Pauling for almost a decade before I accept his invitation to join him as his personal collaborator. Our friendship was built not only on common scientific interests, but also on humanitarian values and the desire to contribute to a better world.

When I decided to leave Germany and join him, he was already 89 years old and was looking for someone to continue his life work in vitamin research and beyond.   He was deeply disappointed about the failure of the institute carrying his name to live up to his expectations in vitamin research and the promotion of nutritional medicine. But at his age he felt too frail to change it on his own.

In 1991 and 1992 Dr. Linus Pauling and I founded two companies in order to provide the funds for vitamin research and to jump start this important process.

AGREEMENT

This is an Agreement between Dr. Matthias Rath and the Linus Pauling Institute of Science and Medicine (LPI), located at 440 Page Mill Road, Palo Alto, California 94306.

Dr. Rath joined LPI in Palo Alto in February 1990.

Dr. Rath brought to LPI the research project on cardiovascular diseases, vitamin C and Lipoprotein(a) and further pursued this program at LPI.

It is mutually understood that this research project was originated by and belongs to Dr. Rath. LPI has greatly benefited from this project with respect to an improvement in its reputation, as well as its financial support.

It is agreed that the Linus Pauling Institute waives to Dr. Rath all interests in this project and the work of Dr. Rath during his employment at LPI. This waiver includes all research data, patent rights, publications, intellectual property and material and non-material issues of any kind.

It is understood that Dr. Rath will further develop this project and thereby continue the life work of Dr. Linus Pauling.

This Agreement supersedes all previous agreements between the parties on this issue.

This Agreement shall be construed and take effect in accordance with the laws of the State of California.

22 July 1992
Date

Dr. Linus Pauling
President and
Chairman, Board of Trustees
Linus Pauling Institute

7/22/92
Date

Stephen D. Maddox
Managing Director
Linus Pauling Institute

7/22/92
Date

Dr. Matthias Rath

Left:
- *Acknowledgment and Assignment of Intellectual Property.*
- *Request to Continue the Life Work of the Nobel Laureate.*

Below:
The Ultimate Trust: Assignment of Dr. Pauling's Very Own Name

---

ASSIGNMENT OF RIGHTS IN NAME AND LIKENESS

1. **Assignment.** Effective 3/12, 1992, Linus Pauling ("Assignor") residing at _Salmon Creek #15,_ _Big Sur, Ca 93920_ hereby assigns to Linus Pauling Health, Inc. located at _440 Page Mill Road, Palo Alto, Ca 94306_ ("Assignee"), its successors, assigns and nominees, all worldwide right, title and interest in the name, voice, signature, endorsement, photographs, visual representations, trademarks, trade names and service marks of Assignor, including but not limited to the trademarks LINUS PAULING, PAULING, DR. LINUS PAULING and PROFESSOR LINUS PAULING (the "Name and Likeness"), together with the business goodwill attributable to or identified with the Name and Likeness, including but not limited to the right to commercial exploitation, publicity, and other proprietary rights in such Name and Likeness, for the full duration of all such rights and renewals or extensions thereof, in exchange for the good and valuable consideration set forth below. Assignor further agrees that it waives its privacy rights in, and consents to the use of, the Name and Likeness in advertising, publicizing or otherwise commercializing Assignee's products (the "Products").

6. **Governing Law.** This Assignment shall be governed by the laws of the State of California, without reference to conflict of laws principles. For any dispute arising under this Assignment, the parties consent to the personal jurisdiction of the state and federal courts within Santa Clara County, California.

Linus Pauling Health, Inc.

By: _____

Name: _Matthias Rath_
          (Print)

Title: _President_

Date: _3/11/92_

Linus Pauling

_____

Date: _3/12/92_

Obstacles in Continuing the Life Work of the Nobel Laureate

The historic failure of the Linus Pauling Institute?

- From its foundation in 1973 until 1990 the Linus Pauling Institute had received over 40 million dollars in public donations. Tens of thousands of small donors gave their money because they were made believe that they support vital vitamin research.
- However, less than ten percent of the money was actually spent for nutritional research. These donations were primarily used for research unrelated to vitamins and for other purposes.
- Dr. Linus Pauling never had the support of his family for his interest in nutrition. Vitamins were too controversial and his children were planning to close the Institute after his demise.

Who was responsible for these misappropriations?

- The Nobel Laureate's son, Linus Pauling *Junior*, a retired psychiatrist from Hawaii, watched and controlled the Board of his fathers Institute over 20 years. The records of its Board of Trustees document that it was Linus *Junior* who personally blocked the following projects of his father for his Institute:
  - the planning and conduct of clinical studies with vitamins
  - the extension of vitamin research
  - the project of a modern nutritional research institute
  - the establishment of a vitamin treatment center.
- Thus, it was the Nobel Laureate's own family who torpedoed life-saving vitamin research at the Linus Pauling Institute over 20 years. While the pharmaceutical companies were openly fighting vitamins, the most important *independent* research institute was paralized from within. As a consequence, millions of people continued to die from heart disease and other preventable diseases.

Continued obstruction of the life-work of Linus Pauling

- In 1990, at age 89, the Nobel Laureate finally realized that his ideals had been buried during his lifetime. He invited Dr. Rath and asked him to continue his life work. In order to jump-start this process, the two scientists founded two companies to create the revenues for vital vitamin research.
- When the family of the Nobel Laureate found out about these efforts, they organized a coup. In July 1992, Linus Pauling *Junior* replaced his father as president and chairman of the Linus Pauling Institute. The audio tape recordings of this historic Board meeting became public. On it, Linus Pauling *Junior* announces: "As the result of a *Palace Revolution* I became Chairman of the Institute."
- Dr. Rath left this Institute because his research was too important to be compromised by family controversies. He founded Health Now, a research firm in Nutritional and Cellular Medicine.

Selling the name of the Nobel Laureate for personal gain
- By 1993 the Nobel Laureate was bedridden with prostate cancer. Nevertheless, his heirs decided to market his name for profit. They hired a corporate law firm, Cooley, Godward, Huddleson & Tatum of Palo Alto to launch their own company, named LCProgeny.
- Subsequently, they entered into an agreement with the cosmetic firm *Elizabeth Arden* to market Linus Pauling skin care(!) products. The terminally sick Nobel Laureate was scheduled to appear in TV ads with fashion models. *Elizabeth Arden* soon dropped this dubious collaboration. They had also found out that Linus Pauling *Junior* was a sexual harasser, who had been reprimanded for his behaviour by the Medical Association of the State of Hawaii.
- Violating agreements, the heirs of Dr. Pauling also claimed Dr. Raths work on cardiovascular disease for personal gain, forcing him to defend it.

The Last Will of Nobel Laureate Linus Pauling
- In June 1994, only weeks before his death, the testimony of the Dr. Pauling was taken. Under oath he reaffirmed that these important discoveries were made by Dr. Rath and that he had never worked on heart disease before he met Dr. Rath.
- When asked about his designated successor, the Nobel Laureate testified,"There is no doubt in my mind that I was thinking about Dr. Rath as my successor." This was his last will.
- During this testimony, Dr. Pauling was also questioned by an attorney from *Cooley Godward*, the same law firm promoting LCProgeny. In a conflict of interest, attorney Daniel Johnson falsely pretended that he represents the Nobel Laureate and tried to mislead him in his testimony. When the Nobel Laureate realized this scheme, he testified that he had never seen this attorney!

Lessons to be learned for history
Today, Linus Pauling's family can no longer afford a public role and operates indirectly through front organizations. If you hear about a foundation, university department, institute or a simple vitamin peddler using Linus Pauling's name, you are dealing with the people described on these pages.

Before long, the heirs of Linus Pauling will face charges for misappropriation of millions of dollars in public research funds for obstructing life-saving research over decades, and for causing directly or indirectly the premature death of millions of people – crimes against humanity.

All the facts are public. Scientific historians and everyone interested can review details under CV 738888, Superior Court of San Jose, California, USA.

Eradicating Diseases: Support from the President

In September 1995 I met President Clinton. During the brief encounter I gave him a copy of my book and a copy of the letter documented on the opposite page.

In this letter I encouraged the President of the most powerful nation in the world to use his leadership in support of the eradication of cardiovascular disease. The analogy with President Kennedy's program to conquer the moon was well chosen. A project of the magnitude of eradicating the number one killer of our time requires not only commitment of the people but also the support of the government.

Finally, in June 1997, President Clinton announced a ten-year plan to develop a vaccine against AIDS. The goal was clear: the eradication of the epidemic. In his speech, President Clinton referred to President Kennedy's vision in much the same way as I had encouraged him to do.

Apparently, the President decided not to challenge the pharmaceutical industry in its most lucrative market at that time – cardiovascular drugs. But he picked up on the most important point: The focus on *prevention* and *eradication* of diseases - as opposed to the expansion of a pharmaceutical drug market that keeps diseases ongoing.

The following page documents the Open Letter which I sent to the Heads of States of leading countries in August 1997 urging them to take a firm stand on the most critical issue of free health information:

In September 1995 Dr. Rath met President Clinton. Together with his book he gave him the following letter:

Dear Mr. President:

This book is a contribution to health care reform in America. A successful health care reform should combine both administrative changes and a reform of health care and medicine itself. The scientific concept of Cellular Medicine provides the rationale for an effective health care reform by improving human health and significantly lowering health care costs.

Mr. President, in 1961 President Kennedy announced the audacious aim for man to set foot on the moon. When this goal was achieved by courageous leadership and by the efforts of many, it had united all mankind. The next great mission uniting all mankind is the control of cardiovascular disease, the number one killer in the industrialized world. The scientific rationale and clinical evidence for natural prevention and treatment of cardiovascular diseases, based on essential nutrients, is already reasonably convincing.

With this book I am inviting you to support this important mission. With your leadership and political support, the control of the cardiovascular epidemic can be achieved many years earlier.
Sincerely yours,

Matthias Rath, M.D.

Dr. Rath's Open Letter to the Heads of State

Promote Health Benefits of Vitamins to Control Common diseases and Save Millions of Lives

The course of human events has reached a critical point: Recent scientific advances enable mankind to rid itself of today's most common health problems. We know that heart attacks and strokes are not actual diseases but the direct consequence of long-term vitamin deficiencies that damage the artery walls similar to scurvy. Promoting the health benefits of vitamins and other natural therapies will lead to the control of diseases affecting millions of people world-wide, including heart attacks, strokes, circulatory problems in diabetes, high blood pressure, heart failure, and arrhythmia, most forms of cancer, Alzheimer's disease and many others. The scientific breakthroughs in the area of natural, non-patentable therapies will inevitably replace a multi-billion dollar market of less effective, less safe, but more expensive pharmaceutical drugs.

In order to keep a multi-billion-drug market artificially alive, the pharmaceutical companies of the world have formed a Cartel to block any health information in connection with natural therapies. I am bringing this urgent matter to your attention because you, as the political leader of your country, now have two options: either to surrender to an industry that keeps diseases artificially alive for financial gain, or to promote the eradication of diseases, improve the health of your citizens, and free your national economy from the burden of exploding health care costs.

Over recent years, I have been privileged to lead the scientific breakthrough towards control of cardiovascular disease. The attached clinical study proves unequivocally that coronary artery disease, the cause of heart attacks, can be stopped and reversed naturally, without surgery and angioplasty. Further compelling clinical documentation is contained in my book *Why Animals Don't get Heart Attacks - But People Do*, and on our Internet Pages.

The health benefits and economic advantages for your countrymen as well as for your government are compelling:

· **The People**: Millions of people will directly benefit by liberating themselves from the fear of today's most common causes of suffering and death. The average life expectancy will increase by many years, and enjoying maturity in good health will be the rule, not the exception.

· **Corporations**: Large and small corporations will immediately benefit by significantly reducing health care expenses for their employees. No corporation will be able to stay economically competitive and not take advantage of these natural health breakthroughs.

· **Government**: All levels of the public sector will benefit from health care savings. Trillions of dollars will be saved each year worldwide.

It is inevitable that a market of largely unnecessary pharmaceutical drugs will be cut back at the same rate as the breakthroughs in natural health are spreading. To secure their worldwide markets and financial privileges, the Cartel of pharmaceutical multinationals is leading a global campaign against the health interests of millions of people at all levels:

· At the level of the United Nation's World Trade Organization (WTO), a "Codex Alimentarius Commission" tries to ban all health information in connection to vitamins and other natural therapies.

258

· Under camouflage terms "standardization" and "internationalization" the national and international laws are pushing to outlaw natural health information at the regional level, e.g. through the European Union.
· Led by the German government, an effort is being made through the United Nation's Organization for Economic Cooperation and Development (OECD) to ban health information on the Internet. Under the camouflage of protecting children from unsuitable information, the pharmaceutical companies are creating the legal framework to outlaw dissemination of natural health information on the Internet.
· The governments of large and small nations alike are put under political and economic pressure of pharmaceutical multinationals using lobbyists and subsidiary companies in many countries of the world.

Spearheading these unethical efforts are the German multinationals BASF, Bayer and Hoechst under the political auspices of the German government. Once before in this century, these three companies formed a Cartel, IG Farben, which brought misery and death to millions of people. BASF, Bayer and Hoechst financed the election campaign of Hitler's Nazi Party and, in return, were invited to participate in the plundering of Austria, Czechoslo-vakia, Poland, Norway, Holland, Belgium, France and the rest of Central Europe. In 1947 the Nuremberg War Tribunal convicted 24 BASF, Bayer and Hoechst executives for mass murder and other crimes against humanity.

Until the late 1970's the board chairmen of BASF, Bayer and Hoechst, were all ex-members of the Nazi party. As for former Chancellor Kohl, from 1957 to 1967 the largest German Chemical and Pharmaceutical Association (VCI) employed him as a lobbyist. With the financial help of this association, he became chancellor of Germany and continued to serve their interests.

For a second time in this century the same special interest groups are about to enrich themselves at the expense of the health and lives of hundreds of millions of people worldwide. This must not happen.

On behalf of the people of your country and the world, I am urging you to:
· **Terminate any participation of your country, public or private, in the "Codex Alimentarius" Commission, and other efforts organized within the United Nations in the interest of the pharmaceutical industry to withhold life-saving health information for millions of people,**
· **Oppose any legislation nationally and internationally that limits free access to information on the health benefits of vitamins and other natural therapies,**
· **Support through public health programs and other measures, the use of vitamins and other natural therapies as effective, safe and affordable alternatives to prescription drugs.**
· **Support a health care focus on prevention and eradication of diseases and prohibit the obstruction of these efforts by pharmaceutical companies.**

Tens of thousands of people in our international health network are ready to collaborate with your government to develop and implement public health strategies towards the goal of controlling today's most common diseases.

I trust that you will give this matter the highest level of priority within your government. Because of the urgency and the direct concern to millions of people, I am considering this letter as an Open Letter.

    Sincerely yours,   *Matthias Rath, M.D.*

JOURNAL OF APPLIED NUTRITION, VOLUME 48, NUMBER 3   ORIGINAL REPORT

Nutritional Supplement Program Halts Progression of Early Coronary Atherosclerosis
Documented by Ultrafast Computed Tomography

Matthias Rath, M.D. and Aleksandra Niedzwiecki, Ph.D.

ABSTRACT: The aim of this study was to determine the effect of a defined nutritional supplement program on the natural progression of coronary artery disease. This nutritional supplement program was composed of vitamins, amino acids, minerals, and trace elements, including a combination of essential nutrients patented for use in the prevention and reversal of cardiovascular disease. The study was designed as a prospective intervention before-after trial over a 12 month period and included 55 outpatients age 44-67 with various stages of coronary heart disease. Changes in the progression of coronary artery calcification before and during the nutritional supplement intervention were determined by Ultrafast Computed Tomography (Ultrafast CT). The natural progression rate of coronary artery calcification before the intervention averaged 44% per year. The progression of coronary artery calcification decreased on average 15% over the course of one year of nutritional supplementation. In a subgroup of patients with early stages of coronary artery disease, a statistically significant decrease occurred, and no further progression of coronary calcification was observed. In individual cases, reversal and complete disappearance of previously existing coronary calcifications were documented. This is the first clinical study documenting the effectiveness of a defined nutritional supplement program in halting early forms of coronary artery disease within one year. The nutritional supplement program tested here should be considered an effective and safe approach to prevention and adjunct therapy of cardiovascular disease.

Key words: Coronary heart disease, Ultrafast Computed Tomography, nutritional supplements

INTRODUCTION

According to the World-Health Organization, over 12 million people die every year from heart attacks, strokes and other forms of cardiovascular disease.[1] The direct and indirect costs for treatment of cardiovascular disease are the single largest health care expense in every industrialized country of the world. Despite modest success in some countries in lowering the mortality rate from heart attacks and strokes, the cardiovascular epidemic is still expanding on a worldwide scale.

Current concepts of the pathogenesis of cardiovascular disease focus on elevated plasma risk factors damaging the vascular wall and thereby initiating atherogenesis and cardiovascular disease.[2-4] Accordingly, drugs lowering cholesterol and modulating other plasma risk factors have become a predominant therapeutic approach in the prevention of cardiovascular disease.

A new scientific rationale about the initiation of atherosclerosis and cardiovascular disease was proposed by one of us[5,6] It can be summarized as follows: cardiovascular disease is primarily caused by chronic deficiencies of vitamins and other essential nutrients with defined biochemical properties, such as coenzymes, cellular energy carriers, and antioxidants.[7,8] Chronic depletion of these essential nutrients in endothelial and vascular smooth muscle cells impairs their physiological function. For example, chronic ascorbate deficiency, similar to early scurvy, leads to morphological

impairment of the vascular wall and endothelial microlesions, histological hallmarks of early atherosclerosis. [9-11] Consequently, atherosclerotic plaques develop as the result of an overcompensating repair mechanism comprising deposition of systemic plasma factors as well local cellular responses in the vascular wall.[5,6] This repair mechanism is primarily exacerbated at sites of hemodynamic stress, explaining the predominantly local development of atherosclerotic plaques in coronary arteries and myocardial infarction as the most frequent clinical manifestation of cardiovascular disease.

Animal studies have confirmed this scientific rationale resulting in patents for the combination of ascorbate with other essential nutrients in the prevention and treatment of cardiovascular disease.[12] Based on this patented technology, we have developed a nutritional supplement program, which was tested in this study in patients with coronary heart disease.

SUBJECTS AND METHODS

Patients

A total of 55 patients, 50 men and 5 women, with documented coronary artery disease assessed by Ultrafast CT, were recruited for the study. The inclusion criterion was the availability of a high quality Ultrafast CT scan from a previous visit to the Heart Scan facility in South San Francisco. At the beginning of the study each patient completed a comprehensive questionnaire, which was updated after six months and after 12 months. This questionnaire included medical history, previous cardiac events, and cardiovascular risk factors, as well as individual life style data. Specific questions related to the patients' regular diet, such as strictly vegetarian diet, predominantly fruits and vegetables, predominantly meat, fish or poultry; the daily intake of different vitamins and other essential nutrients; and the frequency of physical exercise by the patient. The laboratory tests available documented a heterogeneous population with respect to plasma cholesterol and triglycerides. About half of the patients were taking different types of prescription medication, including calcium antagonists, nitrates, betablockers, and cholesterol-lowering drugs. Before entering the study, the patients were instructed not to change their diet or lifestyle other than adding the nutritional supplement program tested. Any changes were to be documented in their questionnaires. Compliance with the nutritional supplement program was monitored in the questionnaires, through telephone calls and during the control visits.

Composition and Administration of Nutritional Supplement Program

The following daily dosages of nutritional supplements were taken for a period of one year: Vitamins: Vitamin C 2700 mg, Vitamin E(d-Alpha-Tocopherol) 600 IU, Vitamin A (as Beta-Carotene) 7,500 IU, Vitamin B-1 (Thiamine) 30 mg, Vitamin B-2 (Riboflavin) 30 mg, Vitamin B-3 (as Niacin and Niacinamide) 195 mg, Vitamin B-5 (Pantothenate) 180 mg, Vitamin B-6 (Pyridoxine) 45 mg, Vitamin B-12 (Cyanocobalamin) 90 mcg, Vitamin D (Cholecalciferol) 600 IU. Minerals: Calcium 150 mg, Magnesium 180 mg, Potassium 90 mg, Phosphate 60 mg, Zinc 30 mg, Manganese 6 mg, Copper 1500 mcg, Selenium 90 mcg, Chromium 45 mcg, Molybdenum 18 mcg. Amino acids: L-Proline 450 mg, L-Lysine 450 mg, L-Carnitine 150 mg, L-Arginine 150 mg, L-Cysteine 150 mg. Coenzymes and other nutrients: Folic Acid 390 mcg, Biotin 300 mcg, Inositol 150 mg, Coenzyme Q-10 30 mg, Pycnogenol 30 mg, and Citrus Bioflavonoids 450 mg. Further information at: www.drrath.com

Monitoring of Coronary Artery Disease

The extent of coronary calcification was measured non-invasively with an Imatron C-100 Ultrafast CT scanner in the high-resolution volume mode, using a 100- millisecond exposure time. ECG triggering was used so that each image was obtained at the same point in the diastole, corresponding to 80% of the RR interval. In each scan, 30 consecutive images were obtained at 3-mm intervals beginning 1 cm below the carina and progressing caudally to include the entire length of the coronary arteries. The scans at study entry and after 6 and 12 months of the study included a second scan sequence of 30 images at 3 mm intervals across the entire heart. The 30 images of the second scan were taken between the 3 mm intervals of the first scan resulting in a scanning of the heart at an interval of 1.5 mm. Total radiation exposure using this technique was <1 rad per patient (<.01 Gy).

The scan threshold was set at 130 Hounsfield units (Hu) for identification of calcified lesions. The minimum area to differentiate calcified lesions from CT artifact was 0.68 mm². The lesion score, also designated Coronary Artery Scanning (CAS) score, was calculated by multiplying the lesion area by a density factor derived from the maximal Hounsfield unit within this area.[13] The density factor was assigned in the following way: 1 for lesions with a maximal density with 130-199 Hu, 2 for lesions with 200-299 Hu, 3 for lesions with 300-399 Hu and 4 for lesions > 400 Hu. The total calcium areas and CAS scores of each Ultrafast CT scan were determined by summing individual lesion areas or scores from the left main, left anterior descending, circumflex, and right coronary artery.

Several studies have confirmed an excellent correlation of the extent of coronary artery disease as assessed by Ultrafast CT scanning when compared to angiographic and histomorphometric methods.[13-15] Considering the accuracy and the non-invasive approach, Ultrafast CT was the method of choice for an intervention study that included early, asymptomatic stages of coronary artery disease.

Statistical Analysis

Tabel1: Clinical data of study participants from patient protocol at study onset

		all Patients (n=55)		patients with starting coronary sclerosis (n=21)	
age:	40-49	5	(9%)	4	(8%)
	50-59	24	(44%)	8	(40%)
	60-69	26	(47%)	9	(52%)
smoker		4	(7%)	1	(5%)
ex-smoker		36	(65%)	12	(57%)
diabetic		4	(7%)	0	(0%)
pancreas failure		3	(5%)	1	(5%)
heart attack		5	(9%)	0	(0%)
Angioplasty, balloon catheter		2	(4%)	1	(5%)
use of medication		27	(49%)	7	(33%)
use of vitamin		36	(65%)	15	(71%)

The growth rate of coronary calcifications was calculated as the quotient of the differences in the calcification areas or CAS scores between two scans divided by the months between these scans according to the formula (Area2-Area1):(Date2-Date1), or (CAS score2-CAS score1):(Date2-Date1) respectively. The data were analyzed using standard formulas for means, medians, and standard error of the means (SEM). Pearson's correlation coefficient was used to determine the association between continuous variables. One tailed Student t-test was used to analyze differences between mean values, with a significance defined at <0.5. Progression of calcification was predicted by linear extrapolation. The distribution of the growth rate of CAS scores was described by a smooth curve resulting from a third order polyminal fit ($y = a + bx^3$, where $a = 0.9352959$, $b = 8.8235 \times 10^{-5}$).

RESULTS

The aim of this study was to determine the effect of a defined nutritional supplement program on the natural progression of coronary artery calcification particularly in its initial stages as measured by Ultrafast CT. We therefore evaluated the results of the entire study group (n=55) and of a subgroup of 21 patients with early coronary artery calcification, as defined by a CAS score of <100.

Table 2 separately lists the characteristics of the study population assessed by the questionnaire for all patients and for a subgroup with early coronary artery disease.

This is the first intervention study using Imatron's Ultrafast CT technology. One of the first aims of this study was to determine the rate of natural progression of coronary calcium deposits *in situ* , without the intervention of the nutritional supplement program. Figure 1 shows the distribution of the monthly progression of calcifications in the coronary arteries of all 55 patients in relation to their CAS score at study entry.

We found that the higher the CAS score was initially, without intervention, the faster the coronary calcification progressed. Accordingly, the average monthly growth rate of coronary calcifications ranged from 1 CAS score per month in patients with early coronary heart disease to more than 15 CAS score per month in patients with advanced stages of coronary calcifications. The growth pattern of coronary calcifications can be described as a third order polynomial fit curve. The exponential shape of this curve signifies a first quantification of the aggressive nature of coronary atherosclerosis and emphasizes the importance of early intervention.

The changes in the natural progression rate of coronary artery calcification before the nutritional supplement program (-NS) and after one year on this program (+NS) are shown in Figure 2. The results are presented separately for the calcified area and the CAS score.

As presented in Figure 2.a. the average monthly growth of calcified areas for all 55 patients decreased from 1.24 mm²/month (SEM +/- 0.3) before the nutritional supplement program (-NS) to 1.05 mm²/month (+/- 0.2) after one year on this program (+NS). For patients with early coronary artery disease (Figure 2b), the average monthly growth of the calcified area decreased from 0.49 mm²/month (+/- 0.16) before taking the nutritional supplements (-NS) to 0.28 mm²/month (+/- 0.09) after one year on this program (+NS).

As shown in Figure 2.c the average monthly changes in the total CAS score (calcified area X density

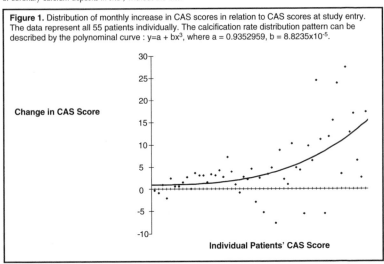

Figure 1. Distribution of monthly increase in CAS scores in relation to CAS scores at study entry. The data represent all 55 patients individually. The calcification rate distribution pattern can be described by the polyminal curve : $y = a + bx^3$, where $a = 0.9352959$, $b = 8.8235 \times 10^{-5}$.

Change in CAS Score

Individual Patients' CAS Score

of calcium deposits) for all 55 patients had decreased after one year on the nutritional supplement program by 11%, from 4.8 CAS score/month (SEM +/-0.97) before the program (-NS) to 4.27 CAS score /month(+/-0.87) (+NS). In patients with early coronary artery disease (Figure 2.d) the average monthly growth of the total CAS score decreased during the same time by as much as 65%, from 1.85 CAS score /month (+/-0.49) before the nutritional supplement program   (-NS) to 0.65 CAS score /month (+/- 0.36) on this program (+NS). The slow-down of the progression of coronary calcification during this nutritional supplement intervention for CAS patients with early coronary artery disease was statistically significant (p<0.05)(Figure 2.d). For the other three sets of data the decrease of coronary calcifications with the nutritional supplement program was evident; however, largely due to the wide range of calcification values at study entry reflecting the different stages of coronary artery disease, it did not reach statistical significance.

It is noteworthy that the decrease in the CAS scores during intervention with nutritional supplements were more pronounced than for the calcified areas. This indicates a decrease in the density of calcium in addition to a reduction in the area of coronary calcium deposits during nutritional supplement intervention.

Ultrafast CT scans at the beginning of the study and after 12 months on the nutritional supplement program, were complemented by a control scan after 6 month,

allowing for additional insight into the time required for the nutritional supplements to exert their therapeutic effect. This additional evaluation was particularly important for early forms of coronary artery disease, because any therapeutic approach that can halt progression of early coronary calcification would ultimately prevent myocardial infarctions.

Figure 3 shows the average coronary calcification areas (Figure 3.a) and total CAS scores (Figure 3.b) for patients with early coronary artery disease measured during different scanning dates before and during the course of the study. The actual coronary calcification values for areas and total CAS scores during nutritional supplement intervention are compared to the predicted values obtained from linear extrapolation of the growth rate without intervention. The letters A to D mark the different time points at which Ultrafast CT scans were performed. AB represents the changes in coronary calcification before intervention with nutritional supplement for the areas (Figure 3.a) and CAS scores (Figure 3.b). Accordingly, BC represents calcification changes during the first six months on the nutritional supplement program and CD changes during the second six months on the program. The calculated progression rate for coronary calcifications without therapeutic intervention by the nutritional supplement program is marked by a dotted line (B through F).

As seen in Figure 3.a without the nutritional supplement program, the average area of coronary calcifica-

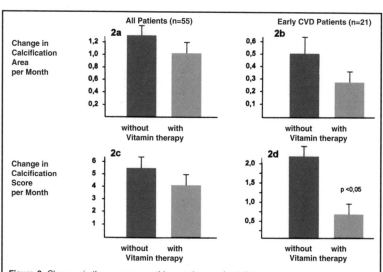

Figure 2. Changes in the average monthly growth rate of calcified areas (2.a,b) and CAS scores (2.c,d) in all study participants (n=55) and in a subgroup of patients with initial stages of coronary calcifications (CAS score<100, n=21), before nutritional supplement intervention (-NS) and after one year of intervention (+NS). Data are mean +/- SEM, asterisk indicates significance at p < 0.05 (one tailed t-test).

263

tions in patients with early coronary artery disease increased from 17.62 mm² (+/- 1.0) at time point A to 23.05 mm² (+/- 1.8) at time point B. Thus, the annual extension of calcified areas without intervention was assessed with 31 %. At this progression rate, the average calcified area would reach 26.3 mm² after six months (point E) and 29.8 mm² after twelve months (point F). The nutritional supplement intervention, resulted in an average calcified area of 25.2 mm2 (+/- 2.2) after six months and of 27.0 mm2 (+/-1.7) after 12 months, reflecting a 10% decrease compared to the predicted value.

Analogous observations were made for the total CAS before and during the nutritional supplement program. Figure 3.b shows that the CAS score before the nutritional supplement program increased by 44% per year, from 45.8 (+/- 3.2) (point A) to 65.9 mm2 (+/- 5.2) (point B). At this progression rate the total CAS score, without the nutritional supplement program, would reach an average of 77.9 after six months (point E) and of 91 (point F) after twelve months. In contrast to this trend the actual CAS score values measured with the nutritional supplement program were 75.8 (+/-6.2) after 6 months (point C) and 78.1 (+/-5.1) after 12 months (point D). Thus, the progression of coronary calcification as determined by the total CAS scores decreased significantly during the second six months of nutritional supplement intervention (CD). The total score after twelve months on the nutritional supplement program was only 3% higher than after six months (CD), as compared to the projected increase of 17% (EF), indicating that during the second six months on the nutritional supplement program the process of coronary cal-

cification has practically stopped.

Figure 4 shows the actual Ultrafast CT scans of a 51 year old patient with early, asymptomatic, coronary artery disease. The patients' first Ultrafast CT scan was performed in 1993 as part of an annual routine checkup. The scan film revealed small calcifications in the left anterior descendent coronary artery as well as in the right coronary artery. The second CT scan was performed one year later at which time the initial calcium deposits had further increased. Figure 4.a shows two Ultrafast CT scan images taken before the nutritional supplement program.

Subsequently, the patient started on the nutritional supplement program. About one year later the patient received a control scan. At this time point, coronary calcifications were not found (Figure 4b), indicating the natural reversal of coronary artery disease.

DISCUSSION

This is the first study that provides quantifiable data from *in situ* measurements about the natural progression rate of coronary artery disease. Although atherosclerotic plaques have a complex histomorphological composition, calcium dispersion within these plaques has been shown to be an excellent marker for their advancement.[11,13] Our study determined that the calcified vascular areas expand at a rate between 5 mm2 (early atherosclerotic lesions) and 40 mm2 (advanced atherosclerotic lesions). Before the nutritional supplement program the average annual increase of total coronary calcification was 44% (Figure 1). Considering the exponential increase of coronary calcification, it is evident that the control of cardiovascular disease has to

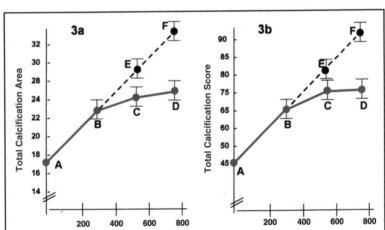

Figure 3. Actual progression of coronary calcification areas and CAS scores before and during one year of nutritional supplement intervention in a subgroup of patients with initial stages of coronary calcification (CAS <100), compared to calculated progression without intervention (dotted line). Each data point represents the mean value +/- SEM.

focus on early diagnosis and early intervention.

Today, the diagnostic assessment of individual cardiovascular risk is largely confined to the measurement of plasma cholesterol and other risk factors with little correlation to the extent of atherosclerotic plaques. More accurate methods, such as coronary angiography, are confined to advanced, symptomatic, stages of coronary artery disease. Ultrafast CT provides the diagnostic option to quantify coronary artery disease non-invasively in its early stages.[14,15]

The most important finding of this study is that coronary artery disease can be effectively prevented and treated by natural means. This nutritional supplement program was able to decrease the progression of coronary artery disease within the relatively short time of one year, irrespective of the stage of this disease. Most significantly, in patients with early coronary calcifications this nutritional supplement program was able to essentially stop its further progression. In individual cases with small calcified deposits, nutritional supplement intervention led to their complete disappearance (Figure 4).

We postulate that the nutritional supplement program tested in this study initiates the reconstitution of the vascular wall. Restructuring of the vascular matrix is facilitated by several nutrients tested, such as ascorbate (vitamin C), pyridoxine (vitamin B-6), L-lysine, and L-proline, as well as the trace element copper. Ascorbate is essential for the synthesis and hydroxylation of collagen and other matrix components,[16-18] and can be directly and indirectly involved in a variety of regulatory mechanisms in the vascular wall from cell differentiation to distribution of growth factors.[19,20] Pyridoxine and copper are essential for the proper cross-linking of matrix components.[8] L-lysine and L-proline are impor-

tant substrates for the biosynthesis of matrix proteins; they also competitively inhibit the binding of lipoprotein(a) to the vascular matrix, facilitating the release of lipoprotein(a) and other lipoproteins from the vascular wall.[5,12,21] Ascorbate and -tocopherol have been shown to inhibit the proliferation of vascular smooth muscle cells.[22-24] Moreover, tocopherols, beta-carotene, ascorbate, selenium and other antioxidants scavenge free radicals and protect plasma constituents, as well as vascular tissue, from oxidative damage.[25,26] In addition, nicotinate, riboflavin, pantothenate, carnitine, coenzyme Q-10, as well as many minerals and trace elements, function as cellular cofactors in form of NADH, NADPH, FADH, Coenzyme A and other cellular energy carriers.[8] The results of this study confirm that maintaining the integrity and physiological function of the vascular wall is the key therapeutic target in controlling cardiovascular disease. This also corroborates early angiographic findings that supplemental vitamin C may halt the progression of atherosclerosis in femoral arteries.[27]

These conclusions are even more relevant since deficiencies of essential nutrients are common.[28,29] Moreover, many epidemiological and clinical studies have already documented the benefits of individual nutrients in the prevention of cardiovascular disease.[30-35] Compared to the high dosages of vitamins used in some of these studies the amounts of nutrients used in this study are moderate, indicating the synergistic effect of this program.

In this context, it seems appropriate to critically review some of the approaches currently used in the primary and secondary prevention of cardiovascular disease, including the extensive use of cholesterol-lowering drugs. An intervention study including lovastatin

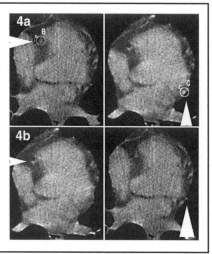

Figure 4. Ultrafast CT scan images of a 50 year old patient with asymptomatic coronary artery disease before the nutritional supplement program (top row) and approximately one year later (bottom row). Calcium deposits in the left descending coronary artery and in the right coronary artery are visible as white areas.

was performed with a highly selected group of hyperlipidemic patients, representing only an extremely narrow fraction of a normal population.[36] More recently, the reduction of myocardial infarctions and other cardiac events in patients taking simvastatin, led to recommendations for its long-term use even by normolipidemic patients.[37] However, because of their potential side-effects, the recommended use of these drugs has now been restricted to patients at high short term risk for coronary heart disease.[38]

Similarly, certain natural approaches to prevention of cardiovascular disease deserve a critical review. A program of rigorous diet and exercise program claims to be able to reverse coronary heart disease.[39] However, the published study does not provide compelling evidence documenting the regression of coronary atherosclerosis. Thus, the improved myocardial perfusion shown in that study, was likely the result of the physical training program, leading to an increased ventricular ejection fraction and an increased coronary perfusion pressure.

Considering the urgent need for effective and safe public health measures towards the control of cardiovascular disease, the validity of this study is of particular importance. In light of this, the following study elements are noteworthy:

1 The patients in this study served as their own controls before and during nutritional supplement intervention, thereby minimizing undesired co-variables such as age, gender, genetic predisposition, diet or medication.

2 Ultrafast CT has been extensively validated to assess the degree of coronary atherosclerosis, and it allowed quantification of coronary atherosclerotic plaques *in situ*.[13-15] This diagnostic technique also minimizes errors as they occur in angiography studies in which vasospasms, formation or lysis of thrombi, and other events cannot be differentiated from progression or regression of atherosclerotic plaques. Moreover, Ultrafast CT provides valuable information about the morphological changes during progression and regression of atherosclerotic plaques, by quantifying not only the area of coronary calcifications but also their density. Furthermore, the automatic CT measurements of coronary calcifications eliminates human error in the evaluation of the data.

In summary, the results of this study imply that coronary heart disease is a preventable and essentially reversible condition. This study documents that coronary artery disease could be halted in its early stages by following this nutritional supplement program. These results were achieved within one year, suggesting that additional therapeutic benefits in patients with advanced coronary artery disease can be obtained by an extended use of this program. The continuation of this study is currently under way to document these effects. This nutritional supplement program signifies an effective and safe approach for the prevention and adjunct therapy of cardiovascular disease. This study should encourage public health policy makers and health care providers to redefine health strategies towards the control of cardiovascular disease.

ACKNOWLEDGEMENTS

We are grateful to Jeffrey Kamradt for his help in coordinating this study. Douglas Boyd Ph.D., Lew Meyer Ph.D. from Imatron/HeartScan., South San Francisco, for helping to plan the study and providing the HeartScan facility; Lauranne Cox, Susan Brody, and Tom Caruso for their collaboration in conducting the heart scans. Dr. Roger Barth and Bernard Murphy for their assistance in planning the study, as well as to Martha Best for her secretarial assistance.

NOTE BY THE AUTHORS

This publication was originally submitted to *the Journal of the American Medical Association* (*JAMA*) on August 5, 1996 and referred to Charles B. Clayman, MD Contributing Editor of *JAMA*, by Editor in Chief, George D. Lundberg, MD.

In his letter dated August 23, 1996, Dr. Clayman rejected publication of this paper without further comments. Apparently the contents of this paper challenged the interests of the pharmaceutical industry and their gatekeepers in the administration of the American Medical association. While thousands of doctors in America and millions of patients were waiting for this life-saving information it was deliberately blocked and sabotaged by special interest groups inside *the American Medical Association.*

The background: This study delivered indisputable proof that heart attacks – the number one killer in America – are vitamin deficiency conditions that can be prevented naturally by an optimum intake of essential nutrients. The publication of this study threatens a multi-billion dollar market in cholesterol-lowering drugs and other unnecessary pharmaceuticals currently marketed for heart conditions.

Following the provocative rejection of this paper by the *American Medical Association Journal's* office, we immediately submitted our manuscript to the *Journal of Applied Nutrition* whose reviewers understood the importance of this study for the health and life of every human being on earth as well as for future generations. They immediately accepted this study for publication.

Following this decision, Dr. Rath received a letter from the *JAMA* office asking for a resubmission of the study for reconsideration of its publication. Apparently, the American Medical Association had realized its grave mistake. But it was too late. The credit for publishing this important study will go forever to the *Journal of Applied Nutrition.*

As for the *American Medical Association,* thousands of doctors in America will have to hold their elected officers responsible for their unethical actions which were taken for no other reason than to serve special interests from the pharmaceutical industry. If the doctors in America do not clean up their house, the American people must see their organization as a puppet of the Pharma-Cartel. If the doctors of America don't act now, the *American Medical Association* will loose all remaining credibility that it serves the health interests of the American people.

REFERENCES

World Health Statistics, World Health Organization, Geneva, 1994.

Brown MS, Goldstein JL. How LDL receptors influence cholesterol and atherosclerosis. *Scientific American* 1984;251:58-66.

Steinberg D, Parthasarathy S, Carew TE, Witztum JL. Modifications of low-density lipoprotein that increase its atherogenicity. *N Engl J Med.* 1989;320:915-924.

Ross R. The pathogenesis of atherosclerosis-an update. *N Engl J Med.* 1986;314:488-500.

Rath M, Pauling L. A unified theory of human cardiovascular disease leading the way to the abolition of this diseases as a cause for human mortality. *J Ortho Med.* 1992;7:5-15.

Rath M, Pauling L. Solution to the puzzle of human cardiovascular disease: Its primary cause is ascorbate deficiency, leading to the deposition of lipoprotein(a) and fibrinogen/fibrin in the vascular wall. *J Ortho Med.* 1991;6:125-134.

Rath M. Reducing the risk for cardiovascular disease with nutritional supplements. *J Ortho Med* 1992;3:1-6.

Stryer I. *Biochemistry*, 3rd ed. New York: W.H.Freeman and Company; 1988.

Stary HC. Evolution and progression of atherosclerotic lesions in coronary arteries of children and young adults. *Atherosclerosis (Suppl.)* 1989;9:I-19-I-32.

Constantinides P. The role of arterial wall injury in atherogenesis and arterial thrombogenesis. *Zentralbl allg Pathol pathol Anat.* 1989;135:517-530

Stolman JM, Goldman HM, Gould BS. Ascorbic acid in blood vessels. *Arch Pathol.* 1961;72:59-68

US Patent #5,278,189

Agatston AS, Janowitz WR, Kaplan G, Gasso J, Hildner F, Viamonte M. Ultrafast computed tomography—detected coronary calcium reflects the angiographic extent of coronary arterial atherosclerosis. *Am J Cardiology.* 1994;74:1272-1274.

Budoff MJ, Georgiou D, Brody A, et al. Ultrafast computed tomography as a diagnostic modality in the detection of coronary artery disease. *Circulation.* 1996; 93:898-904.

Mautner SI, Mautner GC, Froehlich J, et al. Coronary artery disease: prediction with in vitro electron beam CT. *Radiology.* 1994;192:625-630.

Murad S, Grove D, Lindberg KA, Reynolds G, Sivarajah A, Pinnell SR. Regulation of collagen synthesis by ascorbic acid. *Proc Natl Acad Sci.* 1981;78:2879-2882.

De Clerck YA, Jones PA. The effect of ascorbic acid on the nature and production of collagen and elastin by rat smooth muscle cells. *Biochem J.* 1980;186:217-225.

Schwartz E, Bienkowski RS, Coltoff-Schiller B, Goldfisher S, Blumenfeld OO. Changes in the components of extracellular matrix and in growth properties of cultured aortic smooth muscle cells upon ascorbate feeding. *J Cell Biol.* 1982;92:462-470.

Francheschi RT. The role of ascorbic acid in mesenchymal differentiation. *Nutr Rev.* 1992;50:65-70

Dozin B, Quatro R, Campanile g, Cancedda R. In vitro differentiation of mouse embryo chondrocytes: requirement for ascorbic acid. *Eur J Cell Biol.* 1992;58:390-394.

Trieu VN, Zioncheck TF, Lawn RM, McConathy WJ. Interaction of apolipoprotein(a) with apolipoprotein B-containing lipoproteins. *J Biol Chem.* 1991; 226:5480-5485.

Boscoboinik D, Szewczyk A, Hensey C, Azzi A. Inhibition of cell proliferation by -tocopherol. Role of protein kinase C. *J Biol Chem.* 1991; 266:6188-6194.

Ivanov V, Niedzwiecki A. Direct and extracellular matrix mediated effects of ascorbate on vascular smooth muscle cells proliferation. *24th AAA (Age) and 9th Am Coll Clin Gerontol Meeting,* Washington DC, 1994;Oct14-18.

Nunes GL, Sgoutas DS, Redden RA, Sigman SR, Gravanis MB, King SB, Berk BC. Combination of vitamins C and E alters the response to coronary balloon injury in the pig. *Arteriosclerosis, Thrombosis and Vascular Biology.* 1995; 15:156-165.

Retsky KL, Freeman MW, Frei B. Ascorbic acid oxidation product(s) protect human low density lipoprotein against atherogenic modification. Anti- rather than prooxidant activity of vitamin C in the presence of transition metal ions. *J Biol Chem.* 1993;268:1304-1309.

Sies H, Stahl W. Vitamins E and C, -carotene and other carotenoids as antioxidants. *Am J Clin Nutr.* 1995;62(Suppl);1315S-1321S.

Willis GC, Light AW, Gow WS. Serial arteriography in atherosclerosis. *Can Med Ass J.* 1954;71:562-568.

Levine M, Contry-Caritilena C, Wang Y, et al. Vitamin C pharmacokinetics in healthy volunteers: Evidence for a recommended daily allowance. *Proc Natl Acad Sci.* 1996;93:3704-3709.

Naurath HJ, Joosten E, Riezler R. Effects of vitamin B12, folate, and vitamin B6 supplements in elderly people with normal serum vitamin concentrations. *The Lancet.* 1995;346:85-89.

Enstrom JE, Kanim LE, Klein MA. Vitamin C intake and mortality among a sample of the United States population. *Epidemiology.* 1992; 3: 194-202.

Riemersma RA, Wood DA, Macintyre CCA, Elton RA, Gey KF, Oliver MF. Risk of angina pectoris and plasma concentrations of vitamin A, C, and E and carotene. *The Lancet.* 1991;337:1-5.

WHY ANIMALS DON'T GET HEART ATTACKS – BUT PEOPLE DO

Hodis HN, Mack WJ, LaBree L, et al. Serial coronary angiographic evidence that antioxidant vitamin intake reduces progression of coronary artery atherosclerosis. *JAMA.* 1995; 273:1849-1854.

Morrison HI, Schaubel D, Desmeules M, Wigle DT. Serum folate and risk of fatal coronary heart disease. *JAMA.* 1996; 275:1893-1896.

Stephens NG, Parsons A, Schofield PM, et al. Randomised controlled trial of vitamin E in patients with coronary disease: Cambridge Heart Antioxidant Study (CHAOS). *The Lancet.* 1996;347:781-786.

Heitzer T, Just H, Münzel T. Antioxidant vitamin C improves endothelial dysfunction in chronic smokers. *Am Heart Assoc.* 1996;comm:6-9.

Brown BG, Albers JJ, Fisher LD, Schafer SM, Lin J-T, *et al.* Regression of coronary artery disease as a result of intensive lipid-lowering therapy in men with high levels of apolipoprotein B. *N Engl J Med.* 1990;323:1289-1298.

Scandinavian Simvastatin Survival Study Group. Randomised trial of cholesterol lowering in 4444 patients with coronary heart disease: the Scandinavian Simvastatin Survival Study (4S). *The Lancet* 1994;344:1383-1389.

Newman TB, Hulley SB. Carcinogenicity of lipid-lowering drugs. *JAMA.* 1996;275:55-60.

Gould KL, Ornish D, Scherwitz L, et al. Changes in myocardial perfusion abnormalities by positron emission tomography after long-term, intense risk factor modification. *JAMA* 1995;274:894-901.

About the Author

Dr. Rath was born in Stuttgart, Germany, in 1955. After graduating from medical school he worked as a physician and researcher at the University Clinic of Hamburg, Germany and the German Heart Center in Berlin. His research focused on the causes of atherosclerosis and cardiovascular disease. In 1987 Dr. Rath discovered the connection between lipoprotein(a) and vitamin C deficiency. In 1990, he become Director of Cardiovascular Research at the Linus Pauling Institute in California.

In 1992, Dr. Rath founded his own research and development firm in Nutritional and Cellular Medicine. He is the holder of several patents for the natural prevention and treatment of cardiovascular disease. Dr. Rath's scientific publications have appeared in the most reputable journals, including Arteriosclerosis, Proceedings of the National Academy of Sciences, European Heart Journal and others. His popular science books have been translated in ten languages and several hundred thousand copies have been sold.

Dr. Rath's research in the structure and function of proteins led to the discovery of the "Protein Code", the other fundamental biological language beside the "Genetic Code". On the basis of this research direction, vaccines will become available for the biological treatment of advanced cancer and other severe health conditions. The mission of Dr. Rath's research firm differs fundamentally from pharmaceutical companies by focusing exclusively on therapies that prevent and eradicate diseases rather than just alleviating symptoms.

"Fighting for a medical breakthrough against existing interests and dogmas is like sailing on the ocean", says Dr. Rath, "the wind that blows in your face becomes your compass". And he adds: "You don't have to be a university professor or Nobel Laureate to lead a medical breakthrough. The only important thing is that heart attacks, strokes and other diseases of today will be largely unknown in the future."

Dr. Rath comes from a modest background. His parents were farmers in Southern Germany who passed their humanitarian values on to their children. "These values", says Dr. Rath, "are still a driving force for me. My life is an example that you do not have to be born privileged to make a contribution to a better world."

The headquarters of Dr. Rath's research firm is located in Almelo, Holland.

Acknowledgments

My thanks go to all those without whom the medical break-through towards control of cardiovascular disease would be delayed by many years.

My thanks also go to all those who have remained an invaluable source of motivation for me through their skepticism and opposition.

Dr. Matthias Rath

References

The following comprehensive list of references is compiled to document the broad support nutritional and Cellular Medicine already has. You will find these publications in larger public libraries and in the library of any medical school.

Armstrong VW, Cremer P, Eberle E, et al. (1986) The association between serum Lp(a) concentrations and angiographically assessed coronary atherosclerosis. Dependence on serum LDL-levels. Atherosclerosis 62: 249-257.

Altschul R, Hoffer A, Stephen JD. (1955) Influence of nicotinic acid on serum cholesterol in man. Archives of Biochemistry and Biophysics 54: 558-559.

Aulinskas TH, Van Westhuyzen DR, Coetzee GA. (1983) Ascorbate increases the number of low density lipoprotein receptors in cultured arterial smooth muscle cells. Atherosclerosis 47: 159-171.

Avogaro P, Bon G B, Fusello M. (1983) Effect of pantethine on lipids, lipoproteins and apolipoproteins in man. Current Therapeutic Research 33: 488-493.

Bates CJ, Mandal AR, Cole TJ. (1977) HDL. cholesterol and vitamin-C status. The Lancet II: 611.

Beamish R. (1993) Vitamin E - then and now. Canadian Journal of Cardiology 9: 29-31.

Beisiegel U, Niendorf A, Wolf K, Reblin T, Rath M. (1990) Lipoprotein (a) in the arterial wall. European Heart Journal 11 (Supplement E): 174-183.

Berg K. (1963) A new serum type system in man - the Lp system. Acta Pathologica Scandinavia 59: 369-382.

Blumberg A, Hanck A, Sandner G. (1983) Vitamin nutrition in patients on continuous ambulatory peritoneal dialysis (CAPD). Clinical Nephrology 20: 244-250.

Braunwald E, Hrsg. (1992) Heart Disease – A textbook of cardiovascular medicine. W.B. Saunders & Company, Philadelphia.

Briggs M, Briggs M. (1972) Vitamin C requirements and oral contraceptives. Nature 238: 277.

Carlson LA, Hamsten A, Asplund A. (1989). Pronounced lowering of serum levels of lipoprotein Lp(a) in hyperlipidemic subjects treated with nicotinic acid. Journal of Internal Medicine (England) 226: 271-276.

Cherchi A, Lai C, Angelino F, Trucco G, Caponnetto S, Mereto PE, Rosolen G, Manzoli U, Schiavoni G, Reale A, Romeo F, Rizzon P, Sorgente I, Strano A, Novo S, Immordino R. (1985) International Journal of Clinical Pharmacology, Therapy and Toxicology: 569-572.

Chow CK, Changchit C, Bridges RBI, Rein SR, Humble J, Turk J. (1986) Lower levels of vitamin C and carotenes in plasma of cigarette smokers. Journal of the American College of Nutrition 5: 305-312.

Clemetson CAB. (1989) Vitamin C, Volume I-III. CRC Press Inc., Florida.

Cushing GL, Gaubatz JW, Nave ML, Burdick BJ, Bocan TMA, Guyton JR, Weilbaecher D, DeBakey ME, Lawrie GM, Morrisett JD. (1989) Quantitation and localization of lipoprotein (a) and B in coronary artery bypass vein grafts resected at re-operation. Arteriosclerosis 9: 593-603.

Dahlen GH, Guyton JR, Attar M, Farmer JA, Kautz JA, Gotto AM, Jr. (1986) Association of levels of lipoprotein LP(a), plasma lipids, and other lipoproteins with coronary artery disease documented by angiography. Circulation 74: 758-765.

DeMaio SJ, King SB, Lembo NJ, Roubin GS, Hearn JA, Bhagavan HN, Sgoutas DS. (1992) Vitamin E supplementation, plasma lipids and incidence of restenosis after percutaneous transluminal coronary angioplasty (PTCA). Journal of the American College of Nutrition 11: 68-73.

Dice JF, Daniel CW. (1973) The hypoglycemic effect of ascorbic acid in a juvenile-onset diabetic. International Research Communications System: 1: 41.

Digiesi V. (1992) Mechanism of action of coenzyme Q10 in essential hypertension. Current Therapeutic Research 51: 668-672.

England M. (1992) Magnesium administration and dysrhythmias after cardiac surgery: A placebo-controlled, double-blind randomized trial. Journal of the American Medical Association 268: 2395-2402.

Enstrom JE, Kanim LE, Klein MA. (1992) Vitamin C intake and mortality among a sample of the United States population. Epidemiology 3: 194-202.

Ferrari R, Cucchini, and Visioli O. (1984) The metabolical effects of L-carnitine in angina pectoris. International Journal of Cardiology 5: 213-216.

Folkers K, Yamamura Y (Hrsg.). (1976,1979,1981,1984,1986) Biomedical and clinical aspects of coenzyme Q. Volume 1-5. Elsevier Science Publishers, New York.

Folkers K, Vadhanavikit S, Mortensen SA. (1985) Biochemical rationale and myocardial tissue data on the effective therapy of cardiomyopathy with coenzyme Q10. Proceedings of the National Academy of Sciences USA 82: 901-904.

Folkers K, Langsjoen P, Willis R, Richardson P, Xia LJ, Ye CQ, Tamagawa H. (1990) Lovastatin decreases coenzyme Q-10 levels in humans. Proceedings of the National Academy of Sciences USA 87: 8931-8934.

Gaby SK, Bendich A, Singh VN, Machlin LJ (Hrsg.). (1991) Vitamin intake and health. Marcel Dekker Inc. N.Y.

Gaddi A, Descovich GC, Noseda G, Fragiacomo C, Colombo L, Craveri A, Montanari G, Sirtori CR. (1984) Controlled evaluation of pantethine, a natural hypolipidemic compound, in patients with different forms of hyperlipoproteinemia. Atherosclerosis 5: 73-83.

Galeone F, Scalabrino A, Giuntoli F, Birindelli A, Panigada G, Rossi, Saba P. (1983) The lipid-lowering effect of pantethine in hyperlipidemic patients: a clinical investigation. Current Therapeutic Research 34: 383-390.

Genest J Jr., Jenner JL, McNamara JR, Ordovas JM, Silberman SR, Wilson PWF, Schaefer EJ. (1991) Prevalence of lipoprotein (a) Lp(a) excess in coronary artery disease. American Journal of Cardiology 67: 1039-1045.

Gerster H. (1991) Potential role of beta-carotene in the prevention of cardiovascular disease. International Journal of Vitamin and Nutrition Research 61: 277-291.

Gey KF, Stähelin HB, Puska P and Evans A. (1987) Relationship of plasma level of vitamin C to mortality from ischemic heart disease. 110-123. In: Burns JJ, Rivers JM, Machlin LJ (Hrsg.): Third conference on vitamin C. Annals of the New York Academy of Sciences 498.

Gey KF, Puska P, Jordan P, Moser UK. (1991) Inverse correlation between plasma vitamin E and mortality from ischemic heart disease in cross-cultural epidemiology. American Journal of Clinical Nutrition 53: 326, Supplement.

Ghidini O, Azzurro M, Vita A, Sartori G. (1988) Evaluation of the therapeutic efficacy of L-carnitine in congestive heart failure. International Journal of Clinical Pharmacology, Therapy and Toxicology 26: 217-220.

Ginter E. (1973) Cholesterol: Vitamin C controls its transformation into bile acids. Science 179: 702.

Ginter E. (1978) Marginal vitamin C deficiency, lipid metabolism, and atherosclerosis. Lipid Research 16: 216-220.

Ginter E (1991) Vitamin C deficiency cholesterol metabolism and atherosclerosis. Journal of Orthomolecular Medicine 6: 166-173.

Guraker A, Hoeg JM, Kostner G, Papadopoulos NM, Brewer HB Jr. (1985) Levels of lipoprotein Lp(a) decline with neomycin and niacin treatment. Atherosclerosis 57: 293-301.

Halliwell B, Gutteridge JMC (Hrsg.). (1985) Free radicals in biology and medicine. Oxford University Press, London, New York, Toronto.

Harwood HJ Jr, Greene YJ, Stacpoole PW (1986) Inhibition of human leucocyte 3-hydroxy-3-methylglutaryl coenzyme A reductase activity by ascorbic acid. An effect mediated by the free radical monodehydro-ascorbate. Journal of Biological Chemistry 261: 7127-7135.

Hearn JA, Donohue BC, Ba'albaki H, Douglas JS, King SBIII, Lembo NJ, Roubin JS, Sgoutas DS. (1992) Usefulness of serum lipoprotein (a) as a predictor of restenosis after percutaneous transluminal coronary angioplasty. The American Journal of Cardiology 68: 736-739.

Hennekens, C. See: Rimm EB (1993) and Stampfer (1993).

Hermann WJ JR, Ward K, Faucett J. (1979) The effect of toco-pherol on high-density lipoprotein cholesterol. American Journal of Clinical Pathology 72: 848-852.

Hemilä H. (1992) Vitamin C and plasma cholesterol. In: Criti-cal Reviews in Food Science and Nutrition 32 (1): 33-57, CRC Press Inc., Florida.

Hoff HF, Beck GJ, Skibinski CI, Jürgens G, O'Neil J, Kramer J, Lytle B. (1988) Serum Lp(a) level as a predictor of vein graft stenosis after coronary artery bypass surgery in patients. Circulation 77: 1238-1244.

Iseri LT. (1986) Magnesium and cardiac arrhythmias. Magne-sium 5: 111-126.

Iseri LT, French JH. (1984) Magnesium: nature's physiologic calcium blocker. American Heart Journal 108: 188-193.

Jacques PF, Hartz SC, McGandy RB, Jacob RA, Russell RM. (1987) Ascorbic acid, HDL, and total plasma cholesterol in the elderly. Journal of the American College of Nutrition 6: 169-174.

Kamikawa T, Kobayashi A, Emaciate T, Hayashi H, Yamazaki N. (1985) Effects of coenzyme Q-10 on exercise tolerance in chronic stable angina pectoris. American Journal of Car-diology 56: 247-251.

Koh ET (1984) Effect of Vitamin C on blood parameters of hypertensive subjects. Oklahoma State Medical Association Journal 77: 177-182.

Korbut R. (1993) Effect of L-arginine on plasminogen-activator inhibitor in hypertensive patients with hypercholes-terolemia. New England Journal of Medicine 328 [4]:287-288.

Kostner GM, Avogaro P, Cazzolato G, Marth E, Bittolo-Bon G, Qunici GB. (1981) Lipoprotein Lp(a) and the risk for myocardial infarction. Atherosclerosis 38: 51-61.

Langsjoen PH, Folkers K, Lyson K, Muratsu K, Lyson T, Langsjoen P. (1988) Effective and safe therapy with coen-zyme Q10 for cardiomyopathy. Klinische Wochenschrift 66: 583-590.

Langsjoen PH, Folkers K, Lyson K, Muratsu K, Lyson T, Langsjoen P. (1990) Pronounced increase of survival of patients with cardiomyopathy when treated with coenzyme Q10 and conventional therapy. International Journal of Tissue Reactions XIII (3) 163-168.

Lavie CJ. (1992) Marked benefit with sustained-release niacin (vitamin B3) therapy in patients with isolated very low levels of high-density lipoprotein cholesterol and coronary artery disease. The American Journal of Cardiology 69: 1093-1085.

Lawn RM. (1992) Lipoprotein (a) in heart disease. Scientific American. June: 54-60.

Lehr, HA, Frei B, Arfors KE. (1994) Vitamin C prevents cigarette smoke-induced leucocyte aggregation and adhesion to endothelium in vivo. Proceedings of the National Academy of Sciences 91: 7688-7692.

Levine M. (1986) New concepts in the biology and biochemistry of ascorbic acid. New England Journal of Medicine 314: 892-902.

Liu VJ, Abernathy RP. (1982) Chromium and insulin in young subjects with normal glucose tolerance. American Journal of Clinical Nutrition 25: 661-667.

Mann GV, Newton P. (1975) The membrane transport of ascorbic acid. Second Conference on Vitamin C. 243-252. Annals of the New York Academy of Sciences.

Mather HM et al. (1979) Hypomagnesemia in diabetes. Clinical and Chemical Acta 95: 235-242.

McBride PE and Davis JE. (1992) Cholesterol and cost-effectiveness implications for practice, policy, and research. Circulation 85: 1939-1941.

McCarron DA, Morris CD, Henry HJ and Stanton JL. (1984) Blood pressure and nutrient intake in the United States. Science 224: 1392-1398.

McNair P et al. (1978) Hypomagnesemia, a risk factor in diabetic retinopathy. Diabetes 27: 1075-1077.

Miccoli R, Marchetti P, Sampietro T, Benzi L, Tognarelli M, Navalesi R. (1984) Effects of pantethine on lipids and apolipoproteins in hypercholesterolemic diabetic and non-diabetic patients. Current Therapeutic Research 36: 545-549.

Mikami H et al. (1990) Blood pressure response to dietary calcium intervention in humans. American Journal of Hypertension 3: 147-151

Newman TB and Hulley SB (1996) Carcinogenicity of lipid-lowering drugs. Journal of the American Medical Association 275: 55-60.

Niedzwiecki A, Ivanov V. (1994) Direct and extracellular matrix mediated effect of ascorbate on vascular smooth muscle cell proliferation. 24th AAA (Age) and 9th American College of Clinical Gerontology Meeting Washington D.C.

Niendorf A, Rath M, Wolf K, Peters S, Arps H, Beisiegel U, Dietel M. (1990) Morphological detection and quantification of lipoprotein (a) deposition in atheromatous lesions of human aorta and coronary arteries. Virchow's Archives of Pathological Anatomy 417: 105-111.

Nunes GL, Sgoutas DS, Redden RA, Sigman SR, Gravanis MB, King SB, Berk BC. (1995) Combination of Vitamin C and E alters the response to coronary balloon injury in the pig. Arteriosclerosis, Thrombosis and Vascular Biology 15: 156-165.

Opie LH. (1979) Review: Role of carnitine in fatty acid metabolism of normal and ischemic myocardium. American Heart Journal 97: 375-388.

Paolisso G et al. (1993) Pharmacologic doses of vitamin E improve insulin action in healthy subjects and in non-insulin-dependent diabetic patients. American Journal of Clinical Nutrition 57: 650-656.

Paterson JC (1941): Canadian Medical Association Journal 44: 114-120.

Pauling L (1986): How to Live Longer and Feel Better. WH Freeman and Company, New York.

Pfleger R, Scholl F. (1937) Diabetes und vitamin C. Wiener Archiv für Innere Medizin 31: 219-230.

Psaty BM, Heckbert SR, Koepsell TD et. al. (1995) The risk of myocardial infarction associated with antihypertensive drug therapies. Journal of the American Medical Association 274: 620-625.

Rath M, Niendorf A, Reblin T, Dietel M, Krebber HJ, Beisiegel U. (1989) Detection and quantification of lipoprotein (a) in the arterial wall of 107 coronary bypass patients. Arteriosclerosis 9: 579-592.

Rath M, Pauling L. (1990a) Hypothesis: Lipoprotein (a) is a surrogate for ascorbate. Proceedings of the National Academy of Sciences USA 87: 6204-6207.

Rath M, Pauling L (1990b) Immunological evidence for the accumulation of lipoprotein (a) in the atherosclerotic lesion of the hypoascorbemic guinea pig. Proceedings of the National Academy of Sciences USA 87: 9388-9390.

Rath M, Pauling L. (1991a) Solution to the puzzle of human cardiovascular disease: Its primary cause is ascorbate deficiency, leading to the deposition of lipoprotein (a) and fibrinogen/fibrin in the vascular wall. Journal of Orthomolecular Medicine 6: 125-134.

Rath M, Pauling L. (1991b) Apoprotein(a) is an adhesive protein. Journal of Orthomolecular Medicine 6: 139-143.

Rath M., Pauling L. (1992a) A unified theory of human cardiovascular disease leading the way to the abolition of this disease as a cause for human mortality. Journal of Orthomolecular Medicine 7: 5-15.

Rath M, Pauling L. (1992b) Plasmin-induced proteolysis and the role of apoprotein(a), lysine, and synthetic lysine analogs. Journal of Orthomolecular Medicine 7: 17-23.

Rath M. (1992c) Lipoprotein-a reduction by ascorbate. Journal of Orthomolecular Medicine 7: 81-82.

Rath M. (1992d) Solution to the puzzle of human evolution. Journal of Orthomolecular Medicine 7: 73-80.

Rath M. (1992e) Reducing the risk for cardiovascular disease with nutritional supplements. Journal of Orthomolecular Medicine 7: 153-162.

Rath M. (1993c) A new era in medicine. Journal of Orthomolecular Medicine 8: 134-135.

Rath M. (1996) The Process of Eradicating Heart Disease Has Become Irreversible. Journal of Applied Nutrition 48: 22-33.

Rath M., Niedzwiecki A. (1996) Nutritional Supplement Program Halts Progression of Early Coronary Atherosclerosis Documented by Ultrafast Computed Tomography. Journal of Applied Nutrition. 48: 68-78.

Rhoads GG, Dahlen G, Berg K, Morton NE, Dannenberg AL. (1986) Lp(a) Lipoprotein as a risk factor for myocardial infarction. Journal of the American Medical Association 256: 2540-2544.

Riales RR, Albrink MJ. Effect of chromium chloride supplementation on glucose tolerance and serum lipids including high-density lipoprotein of adult men. American Journal of Clinical Nutrition 34: 2670-2678.

Riemersma RA, Wood DA, Macintyre CCA, Elton RA, Gey KF, Oliver MF. (1991) Risk of angina pectoris and plasma concentrations of vitamins A, C, and E and carotene. The Lancet 337: 1-5.

Rimm EB, Stampfer MJ, Ascherio AA, Giovannucci E, Colditz GA, Willett WC. (1993) Vitamin E consumption and the risk of coronary heart disease in men. New England Journal of Medicine 328: 1450-1449.

Rivers JM. (1975) Oral contraceptives and ascorbic acid. American Journal of Clinical Nutrition 28: 550-554.

Rizzon P, Biasco G, Di Biase M, Boscia F, Rizzo U, Minafra F, Bortone A, Silprandi N, Procopio A, Bagiella E, Corsi M. (1989) High doses of L-carnitine in acute myocardial infarction: metabolic and antiarrhythmic effects. European Heart Journal 10: 502-508.

Rudolph Willi (1939) Vitamin C und Ernährung. Enke Verlag Stuttgart.

Salonen JT, Salonen R, Ihanainen M, Parviainen M, Seppänen R, Seppänen K, Rauramaa R. (1987) Vitamin C deficiency and low linolenate intake associated with elevated blood pressure: The Kuopio Ischemic Heart Disease Risk Factor Study. Journal of Hypertension 5 (Supplement 5): S521-S524.

Salonen JT, Salonen R, Seppäneen K, Rinta-Kiikka S, Kuukka M, Korpela H, Alfthan G, Kantola M, Schalch W. (1991) Effects of antioxidant supplementation on platelet function:

a randomized pair-matched, placebo-controlled, double-blind trial in men with low antioxidant status. American Journal of Clinical Nutrition 53: 1222-1229.

Sauberlich HE, Machlin LJ (Hrsg.). (1992) Beyond deficiency: new views on the function and health effects of vitamins. Annals of the New York Academy of Sciences 669.

Smith HA, Jones TC, Hrsg. (1958) Veterinary Pathology.

Sokoloff B, Hori M, Saelhof CC, Wrzolek T, Imai T. (1966) Aging, atherosclerosis and ascorbic acid metabolism. Journal of the American Gerontology Society 14: 1239-1260.

Som S, Basu S, Mukherjee D, Deb S, Choudhury PR, Mukherjee S, Chatterjee SN, Chatterjee IB. (1981) Ascorbic acid metabolism in diabetes mellitus. Metabolism 30: 572-577.

Spittle CR. (1971) Atherosclerosis and vitamin C. Lancet ii, 1280-1281.

Stampfer M. et al. (1993) Vitamin E consumption and the risk of coronary heart disease in women. New England Journal of Medicine 328: 1444-1449.

Stankova L, Riddle M, Larned J, Burry K, Menashe D, Hart J, Bigley R. (1984) Plasma ascorbate concentrations and blood cell dehydroascorbate transport in patients with diabetes mellitus. Metabolism 33: 347-353.

Vital Statistics of the United States, US Department of Health and Human Services, National Center for Health Statistics, 1994.

World Health Statistics, World Health Organization, Genf, 1994.

Stepp W, Schroeder H, Altenburger E. (1935) Vitamin C und Blutzucker. Klinische Wochenschrift 14 [26]: 933-934.

Stryer L. (1988) Biochemistry. 3rd edition. W.H. Freeman and Company New York.

Tarry WC. (1994) L-arginine improves endothelium-dependent vasorelaxation and reduces initial hyperplasia after balloon angioplasty. Arteriosclerosis and Thrombosis 14: 938-943.

Teo KK, Salim Y. (1993) Role of magnesium in reducing mortality in acute myocardial infarction: A review of the evidence. Drugs 46[3]: 347-359.

Thomsen JH, Shug AL, Yap VU et al. (1979) Improved pacing tolerance of the ischemic human myocardium after administration of carnitine. American Journal of Cardiology 43: 300-306.

Turlapaty PDMV, Altura BM. (1980) Magnesium deficiency produces spasms of coronary arteries: relationship to etiology of sudden death ischemic heart disease. Science 208: 198-200.

Virchow R. (1859) Cellularpathologie. Verlag von August Hirschwald, Berlin.

Widman L et al. (1993) The dose-dependent reduction in blood pressure through administration of magnesium: A double-blind placebo controlled cross-over study. American Journal of Hypertension 6: 41-45.

Willis GC, Light AW, Gow WS. (1954) Serial arteriography in atherosclerosis. Canadian Medical Association Journal 71: 562-568.

Zenker G, Koeltringer P, Bone G, Kiederkorn K, Pfeiffer K, Jürgens G. (1986) Lipoprotein (a) as a Strong Indicator for Cardiovascular Disease. Stroke 17: 942-945.

Visit the World's Leading Website on Natural Health:

www.drrath.com

- **Visit the consulting center for Cellular Medicine on the Web.**

- **Find the latest information on vitamin research in the prevention and treatment of cardiovascular diseases and other health problems.**

- **Read chapters from Dr. Rath's books or from landmark health studies.**

- **Digest the latest information about the Pharma-Cartel's struggle to suppress this book and to make vitamins prescription drugs.**

In short: Find everything the Pharma-Cartel does not want you to know.

For more information contact Dr. Rath in:

USA and Canada:
P.O. Box 629 000
El Dorado Hills, CA 95762
Tel: 1-800-624-2442 or 916-939-1003
Fax: 1-800-582-8000 or 916-939-1010

Europe:
MR Publishing Inc.
Postbus 859
7600 AW Almelo
The Netherlands
Tel. (31) 546 533 330
Fax (31) 546 533 344

Branch UK:
MR Publishing Inc.
Liverpool Road
Slough
SL 14 QZ
Fax 017-53 69 00 69
www.rath.co.uk